Impossible-to-Resist
DESSERTS

By the same author
COOKING NATURALLY: Wholefood Cuisine with Flair and Finesse

Impossible-to-Resist DESSERTS

Maria Middlestead

Photography by Chris Lewis

HODDER AND STOUGHTON
AUCKLAND LONDON SYDNEY TORONTO

Dedicated to the 'average' cook
within whom abides an adventurous artist
awaiting release!

Copyright © 1987 Maria Middlestead
First published 1987
ISBN 0 340 401168

All rights reserved. No part of this publication may be reproduced or transmitted in any form or by any means, electronic or mechanical including photocopy, recording, or any information storage and retrieval system, without permission in writing from the publisher.

Design and typesetting by Acorn Graphics Ltd.
Printed and bound in Hong Kong for Hodder and Stoughton Ltd, 46 View Road, Glenfield, Auckland, New Zealand.

Contents

The First Step — 7
understanding your ingredients

Chocolate Pleasures 10
Fruit Fantasies 23
Crème de la Crème — 34
cream, chiffon and custard delights
From the Tea Trolley — 48
elegant cakes and pastries
The Frozen Few 61
Simply Superb — 73
quick and easy glamour desserts
The Finishing Touch — 82
glamorous garnishes

Component Cooking — 84
how to create your own designer originals

Index — 87

Introduction

I know people who have been strict vegetarians since birth, people whose diets might grace a textbook, but I don't think I know anyone who doesn't on occasion submit with a smile to the sweet delight, that ephemeral display of art, science and imagination which a fine dessert can be.

Within this book you find desserts which are special, for events which are special. These light, or rich and heady designer statements are made not to cap off an ordinary meal but to provide the climax for a significant one. If we consume them in moderation, we can still treat our health with respect.

Notation is offered on recipe variations, presentation tips and how to alter ingredients to suit your needs. The magic of Component Cooking is outlined: a simple process which transforms the average cook into an adventurous expert. These largely original recipes feature spectacular results and yet need only straightforward preparation. Each one has been lovingly tested so you can be assured of success.

My panel of tasters has sighed with approval, loudly and at length, and likewise invites you to sample the pleasures herein (I thank them for their unstinting attitude of selfless service). So cook, create, and give multi-dimensional delight to those around you.

Maria Middlestead

The First Step —
understanding your ingredients

Working with Cream
- To whip cream have it well chilled; especially in hot weather it is also wise to use a chilled bowl. For small amounts of cream a large balloon whisk works almost as rapidly as an electric mixer and gives slightly more volume.
- When cream is to be sweetened and flavoured whip it until it has been thickened, then gradually start adding sugar and taste the cream until the desired sweetness is reached. Confectioner's sugar with its 3 per cent cornstarch often helps stabilise cream and keeps it from watering, whereas granulated sugar, with its large water content, tends to melt into the cream and speed the separation process.
- To prepare cream for mousse and bavarians, beat it only until thickened but not stiff. The more air incorporated into the cream, the drier the pudding or mousse will be. It is better to slightly underwhip the cream when a rich, compact texture is required.

Working with Eggs
- Eggs separate best when they are cold. The yolk, which is composed largely of fat, is more solidified when cold and less apt to break.
- After separating eggs, store extra yolks in a glass container and cover them with oil. They will keep a week this way. Store extra whites in the freezer. Freeze each white separately in an ice-cube container, then turn out the cubes and keep them in a plastic bag in the freezer. You will have exact amounts when necessary.
- If a recipe calls for eggs or egg whites at room temperature and you have forgotten to take them out of the refrigerator, simply crack the eggs into a bowl and warm them slightly over gentle heat.
- Some recipes call for eggs at room temperature because egg whites mount into a greater volume when they are somewhat warm and can incorporate air more readily. In a dish which is dependent on eggs for volume, such as souffle and sponge cake, everything you can do to increase volume is worth the effort.
- To beat egg whites, place them in an impeccably clean bowl, particularly without a trace of egg yolk or fat.
- If beaten egg whites are to be folded into a cake batter, mix 1/3 of the recipe's sugar tablespoon by tablespoon with the whites toward the end of their beating. The stiff marshmallow-like whites that result will fold into a batter much more smoothly than plain whites.
- To fold beaten egg whites into a batter, pour the lighter mixture (usually the eggs) on top of the heavier mixture. Using your hands or a rubber spatula, cut down to the bottom then lift up and turn at the same time. Continue cutting through gently but rapidly. Do not overwork as this will decrease the volume of air. Disregard the occasional speck of unincorporated white.

Working with Chocolate
Melting chocolate is a task during which chocolate may well reveal its prima donna character. Overheat it or add mistakenly a speck of water and you will see the chocolate seize up and stiffen with the intransigence of a tantrum-throwing two-year old. To restore harmony try pouring a little oil on the troubled waters: for every 2 tablespoons of chocolate add 1 teaspoon of vegetable oil and beat vigorously until the chocolate behaves itself.

For best results place chocolate in the top of a double boiler or in a smaller pan placed inside a larger one of hot but not boiling water. Make sure the pan holding the chocolate is completely dry and never cover with a lid, or moisture will result. Melt the chocolate slowly then stir until smooth.

- 30 grams (1 oz) of cooking chocolate is equal to 3 tablespoons of cocoa and 1 tablespoon butter or oil.
- If chocolate is to be melted with water, milk, or butter the process is faster and can be done directly over very low heat if stirred and watched carefully.
- The more additives chocolate has (sugar, milk solids, lecithin etc) the more difficult it can be to melt properly. Milk chocolate and others like it should be melted very slowly; grating them first will speed the process.
- White chocolate can be the most difficult to work with. To ensure even melting, grate (firm the chocolate briefly in the freezer if it is at all soft) or finely chop. If white chocolate tightens add a small amount of boiling water and the mixture should smooth itself out.
- Adding alcohol to chocolate, in liqueurs or even in vanilla extract, can sometimes cause chocolate to tighten. Smooth by adding oil or melted butter.

Shaping chocolate
- **Grated chocolate:** for small amounts it can be easiest to scrape or grate chocolate with a vegetable peeler or to cut it finely with a large chef's knife. For a very large amount a food processor with a grating blade may be used, but this is a bother to clean.
- **Chocolate curls:** melt couverture or cooking chocolate and pour onto flat, cool surface, preferably a marble slab, although an Arborite counter top is fine. Using a long, thin metal spatula, spread the chocolate backward and forward until it is a very thin, even layer. Keep working the spatula over the chocolate until the gloss dulls and the chocolate looks as if it is beginning to dry at the edges. Start at the edge. Holding the blade of the spatula at a 45-degree angle, scrape and push against the drying chocolate until it gathers into large curls and rough bark-like pieces. Let the pieces dry until firm, then use as decoration; use a toothpick to pick them up without breaking. These may be stored in an airtight container and kept in a cool place.
- **Chocolate flakes:** melt chocolate and work it as above. Let the chocolate completely harden, then scrape against it with a knife or metal spatula and it will flake into thin shavings.

Random Notes
- For a quickly-made, disposable piping bag (especially good for messy melted chocolate work, or for a fine tip for writing with): roll up a piece of waxed paper into a cone shape. Fill with frosting. Snip off the small end to desired diameter.
- Cookies keep crisper for longer when stored in a jar with crumpled tissue paper on the bottom.
- When a recipe calls for paper to line a baking pan, ordinary brown paper bags (not coloured) may be cut to fit, or save your butter wrappers and use these.

- When measuring an odd-shaped piece of butter that defies the butter wrapper markings, place ample, say 2 cups, water in a large measuring cup and add the butter in chunks until it measures appropriately (e.g. 2½ cups total would mean 2 cups water and ½ cup butter).
- When measuring honey, if oil is used in the recipe, measure that first in the same measuring cup; the honey will later slip out effortlessly.
- Cakes frost best if allowed to sit overnight, but glazes and frostings help a cake retain its freshness. If the exterior of a freshly baked cake seems loose and crumbly, yet you need to frost it promptly, spread on a thin layer of very soft butter, then place the cake briefly in the freezer to harden the coating. Now the frost or glaze will adhere to the smooth surface without picking up crumbs.
- An old-fashioned method for testing cakes to see if they are done is to take the cake from the oven and listen closely. Cooked cakes make no noise; still damp ones sound rather spitty.
- If you have a cake in the oven and forget to time it, the first point at which you can smell the cake indicates that it is close to done. Unlike yeasted bread, a cake batter does not put out an aroma until it becomes firm.
- Place souffles, sponge-type cakes — anything that primarily uses eggs as a leavener — in their baking dishes on top of a baking tray, while baking. This helps diffuse any uneven heat so that batters rise straight and even.

Chocolate Pleasures

Chocolate Truffle Torte

A dramatically presented dressed-up chocolate cake. Two 23cm cakes are baked. One is split into two layers, spread with orange marmalade, and sandwiched with a truffle mixture consisting of the other cake layer crumbled, orange peel, rum and walnuts. Some of this mixture has also been used to form tiny truffles or rum balls which later circle the top of the richly chocolate frosted ensemble. Although the production is simple, the cake does require chilling time overnight. Make use of your COMPONENT COOKING skills and note how this concept is similarly at work in the Viennese Ribbon Cake.

Assembly
Bake and cool the two cakes. While baking soak the currents as indicated. Combine them with the other filling ingredients. Form 12 tiny balls out of the mixture and roll in chocolate sprinkles; refrigerate.

Split one cake into 2 layers and place 1 layer on a serving plate. Cover with half the orange marmalade. Press the remaining truffle filling on top. Cover one side of the other cake layer with marmalade and press this, marmalade side down, onto the filling, keeping the top of the torte as flat as possible. Wrap in foil or cling wrap and chill overnight.

Prepare and chill frosting until of spreading consistency. Cover top and sides of cake with frosting, again keeping the top completely flat. Place truffles around the top edge of the cake. Piped rosettes of whipped cream may first act as a base for the truffles, or fine strands of orange peel may be placed, along with a few chocolate shavings, between each truffle. Chill briefly until frosting is set, or up to 24 hours. Serve.

Chocolate Cake
175 g butter, softened
1½ cups lightly packed brown sugar
2 tbs golden syrup
3 large eggs
⅓ cup hot water
½ cup cocoa
2 cups flour
pinch of salt
2 tsp baking powder
1 tsp baking soda
½ cup sour cream
2 tbs dark rum
Later: 5 tbs fine shred (or finely chopped) orange marmalade

Truffle Filling
½ cup currants
4 tbs dark rum
½ cup finely chopped walnuts
grated rind of 1 large orange
2 tbs orange marmalade
1 cake, crumbled

Chocolate Frosting
90 g butter
¼ cup sour cream
90 g cooking chocolate
1 cup icing sugar
few tablespoons whipped cream or fine strands of orange peel and chocolate shavings

Chocolate Cake
Cream together the butter, sugar and golden syrup. Add the eggs and beat well. Stir the hot water into the cocoa and mix into a paste. Beat into the butter mixture. Stir in dry ingredients alternately with the sour cream and rum. Beat until smooth. Divide batter evenly between two 23cm (9") round cake pans which have been buttered and lined with buttered paper. Bake at 180ºC (350ºF) for 30-35 minutes or until the centre tests dry when pierced with a toothpick. Do not overbake. Remove from tins and cool on racks. (Use the orange marmalade as a spread on both cut surfaces, as indicated above.)

Truffle Filling
Soak the currants in the rum for 2 hours or longer. Stir in the remaining ingredients, with the crumbled cake added last. Blend well.

Chocolate Frosting
Put the butter, chocolate and sour cream in a heatproof bowl and set over hot water until melted. Remove and cool to room temperature. Beat in the icing sugar until smooth. Refrigerate 20 minutes or more until of spreading consistency, adding more icing sugar if necessary. Use the whipped cream, or orange peel and chocolate shavings, as outlined above for a garnish.

Marbled Mocha Bombes

Here sherry-soaked biscuits are sandwiched with mocha cream into rough dome shapes on each dessert plate, then covered with more mocha cream for smoother architectural accuracy. Decorate with whimsy: piped whipped cream around the base studded with dramatic black and white (Black Ball) lollies or more conservative pecans.

Bombes evoke an inviting mystery. They are particularly quick and easy to prepare though they need at least two to four hours chilling time. Optionally the mixture may be shaped into one large log on the serving platter, coated and decorated as before. Serves 5-6.

Assembly
Dip cookies very briefly in sherry. Sandwich cookies generously with an overall total of ⅓ of the mocha cream, creating rough individual dome shapes on each plate (or place them all on a baking tray, transfer and garnish before serving), breaking up cookies as necessary.

Spread remaining mocha cream over each dome to form a smooth and even surface. Decorate as outlined above. Place in freezer for one hour and then refrigerate for one hour if speed is essential, otherwise simply refrigerate for four hours or overnight.

Mocha Cream
In small saucepan combine milk, sugar, coffee and cocoa. Heat gently, stirring constantly until sugar dissolves. Remove from heat and beat in egg yolks. Return to heat, stirring constantly until mixture thickens and coats back of spoon. Cool, then cover and chill.

Beat butter until soft and creamy (make sure your butter is very soft or the mixture will later curdle). Gradually add chilled custard mixture beating constantly until well blended.

Bombes
24 lady fingers or other light, plain biscuit
¼-⅓ cup sherry
whipped cream for garnishing

Mocha Cream
⅔ cup fresh cream or tinned evaporated milk
½ cup sugar
2 tbs instant coffee powder
2 tbs cocoa
2 egg yolks, beaten
250g **very soft** butter

Venus De Milo

A light and lovely lady enhanced by a touch of — Milo! Three layers of crisp, nutty meringue are filled with a simple coffee buttercream. The top is covered with a Milo and cinnamon whipped cream and plenty of toasted almonds. A heavenly, more-ish concoction. Serves 8.

Assembly
While Meringues are baking make and cool Buttercream and Milo Whipped Cream. When Meringues are cool place one on a serving plate and cover with half the buttercream; repeat with Meringue, Buttercream, Meringue. Top with Milo Whipped Cream and cover with the toasted almonds. Refrigerate for 20 minutes or up to several hours.

Almond Meringue
- 4 large egg whites
- ¾ cup icing sugar
- ½ cup sugar
- 2 tbs cornflour
- ⅓ cup ground toasted almonds

Coffee Buttercream
- 4 large egg yolks
- ¾ cup icing sugar
- 2 tbs instant coffee powder
- 2 tbs coffee liqueur (optional)
- ½ cup soft butter

Milo Whipped Cream
- ½ cup cream
- 3 tbs Milo
- ½ tsp cinnamon
- ⅔ cup toasted almonds, medium or finely chopped

Almond Meringue
Beat the egg whites until stiff. Gradually beat in the ½ cup of sugar. Fold in the icing sugar, cornflour and ground almonds.

Meanwhile place brown or baking paper on three baking trays. Draw a 23cm (9") circle on each piece of paper and grease well. Spread meringue evenly on each circle. Bake at 130ºC (250ºF) for about 45 minutes until crisp and dry. Immediately and carefully lift them off the paper and cool meringues on wire racks.

Coffee Buttercream
Beat yolks, icing sugar and coffee powder in a double boiler or bowl over a pan of simmering water, until very thick — mixture will form a ribbon when lifted from the beater or whisk — 3-5 minutes. Remove from heat and stir in liqueur. Cool, then gradually beat in softened butter.

Milo Whipped Cream
Combine cream, Milo and cinnamon and whip until fluffy. Use nuts upon assembly to cover cream.

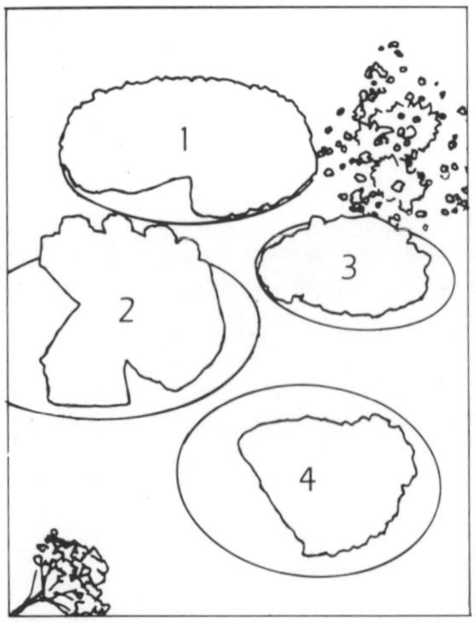

1 Marzipan Mardi Gras (Recipe 13)
2 Chocolate Truffle Torte (Recipe 1)
3 Marbled Mocha Bombe (Recipe 2)
4 Chocolate Cookies & Cream Cake (Recipe 9)

Chocolate Sunset

Something distinctly different for chocolate lovers, this dessert is so named for its dark chocolate background streaked with a glimmer of gold. A dense, moist fudgy cake is completely coated with a smooth, rich Apricot Cream, chilled, then coated again with a solid Chocolate Topping. All three parts are simple and quick to make. The result is stunning.

Assembly
Prepare Apricot Cream; chill. Bake and cool Fudge Cake. Place cake on a large serving plate. Coat top and sides with Apricot Cream. Chill one hour or more until set. Meanwhile prepare and slightly cool Chocolate Topping. Pour Topping evenly over cake in one batch. Working quickly, use a metal spatula to completely smoothe the surface, being careful not to disturb the Apricot Cream. Clean the edges of the plate of any excess chocolate. Surround the bottom cake edge with a border of piped cream and stud at intervals with small slices of tinned or whole dried apricots. Chill until set, one hour or longer.

Apricot Cream
Bring apricots and water to a boil then simmer, uncovered, stirring frequently for 10-15 minutes until completely broken down and a thick puree has formed. Remove from heat and stir in butter. Once melted, stir in remaining ingredients. Cool then refrigerate until very thick and cold.

Fudge Cake
Cream butter and sugar with electric mixer until light and fluffy. Beat in eggs one at a time, beating well after each. Stir or beat in the cocoa and half the flour. Stir in the sour cream. Stir in the remaining flour and baking powder, then the water. Pour into a greased, deep-sided 23cm (9") pan which has its base lined with greased paper. Bake at 180°C (350°F) for 45-50 minutes until a toothpick inserted in the centre comes out clean. Let stand for a few minutes then turn out of the pan onto a wire rack.

Chocolate Topping
Melt chocolate in a bowl over simmering water. Remove from heat and stir in the ½ cup of cream. Allow to cool slightly.

Apricot Cream
- 1½ cups (200g) tart dried apricots
- 1¾ cups water
- 150 g butter, cut into pieces
- ¾ cup icing sugar
- ¼ cup finely diced candied ginger or dried pineapple
- 1 tsp vanilla

Fudge Cake
- 125 g butter, softened
- 1¼ cups sugar
- 2 eggs
- 1 ⅓ cups flour
- ⅓ cup cocoa
- 1 tsp baking powder
- 1 cup sour cream
- ½ cup water

Chocolate Topping
- 200 g cooking chocolate, chopped
- ½ cup cream

For garnishing
- A few tinned or dried apricots
- ½ cup cream, lightly sweetened and whipped for piping

1 Turkish Fig & Chocolate Cake (Recipe 6)
2 Chocolate Sunset (Recipe 4)
3 Lord of the Rings Cake (Recipe 10)

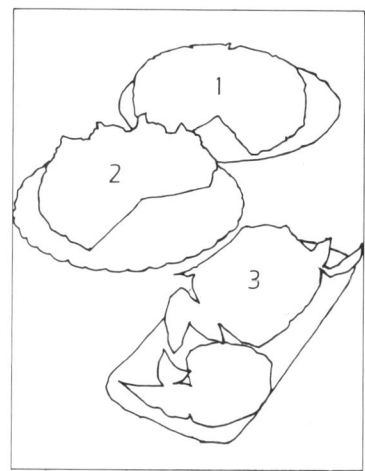

Chocolate Fudge Cake
with Caramelised Walnut Topping

A variation on the previous Chocolate Sunset recipe — that dense fudgy cake is too good to try only once. Here it is coupled with a crisp nutty topping and a light Milo Whipped cream along its sides. Of course the whole combination is a good example of the easy adaptations possible with Component Cooking.

Assembly
Bake cake for 40 minutes. Top with hot Caramelised Walnut Topping and bake a further 10 minutes until Topping is bubbly and a good caramel colour. Cool in pan. Turn out and slide onto a cake plate, nut-side up. Spread sides with Milo Whipped Cream. Chill briefly — or longer — until cream is set. Serve.

Caramelised Walnut Topping
½ cup coarsely chopped walnuts
4 tbs butter
1½ tbs top milk or cream
¼ cup sugar

Fudge Cake
Prepare as for Chocolate Sunset.

Caramelised Walnut Topping
Bring all ingredients to a boil over low heat. Simmer one minute. Use while hot.

Milo Whipped Cream
(See also the Venus de Milo recipe)
½ cup cream
3 tbs Milo
½ tsp cinnamon

Milo Whipped Cream
Combine all ingredients and whip until fluffy.

Turkish Fig & Chocolate Cake

6

Six thin layers of cake are alternately filled with a Spiced Fig Filling and a Chocolate Buttercream. Top and sides are then covered with a patina of melted chocolate. These four aspects to its structure take a little organisation but the result is a large, not too sweet gateau of dramatic appearance. Serve with whipped cream. Serves 12 or more.

Assembly

Prepare Spiced Fig Filling and allow to cool.

Prepare and bake cakes. While they are baking, prepare Chocolate Buttercream.

Place one cake layer on a serving plate and cover with ⅓ of the Fig Filling. Then top with cake, buttercream, cake, fig filling etc., ending with the buttercream and using some of this to frost the sides of the cake as well. Refrigerate until set one hour or longer.

Melt 200 g chocolate over hot water. Pour over top of the chilled cake and working quickly spread lightly over top and sides to completely cover. If this sets before you have finished spreading use a hot dry metal spatula (place under hot water tap; wipe dry) to assist.

Pipe small rosettes of whipped cream around the base and stud alternately with a sliver of dried fig. Serve or chill until serving time. Put remaining cream in a bowl on the table.

Spiced Fig Filling

Bring figs, 1¼ cup water, sugar and mixed spice to a boil, covered. Turn to low and simmer for 10 minutes. Cool to lukewarm and add remaining water and liqueur. Whizz in blender until smooth.

Six-Layer Cake

Cover three baking sheets with brown or baking paper. Trace two 23 cm circles on each sheet. Grease generously.

Allow eggs to come to room temperature. Beat yolks and half the sugar in a medium bowl for 5 minutes or until pale and creamy.

Beat egg whites until stiff. Gradually beat in remaining sugar. Fold into egg yolk mixture. Sprinkle flour over egg mixture and fold in. Spread batter evenly onto greased circles. Bake 6-8 minutes at 220ºC (425ºF) or until a toothpick inserted in the centre comes out clean. Cool for a few minutes on racks then carefully peel off paper. Cool cakes on racks.

Chocolate Buttercream

In small saucepan combine milk, cornflour, sugar and egg yolk. Bring to a boil over medium heat, stirring constantly. Remove from heat when thickened and stir in the 30g of chocolate. Once this is melted stir in the cocoa. Cool to lukewarm.

Cream the butter until smooth. Beat in the chocolate custard a spoonful at a time until well blended.

Spiced Fig Filling
2 cups chopped Turkish figs
1¼ cups water
3 tbs brown sugar
2 tsp mixed spice
⅓ cup cold water
¼ cup Amaretto, Green Ginger Wine, or water with a dash of almond essence

Six-Layer Cake
7 eggs, separated
⅔ cup sugar
1¼ cups flour
1¼ tsp baking powder

Chocolate Buttercream
1 cup milk
3 tbs cornflour
3 tbs sugar
1 egg yolk
30 g cooking chocolate
heaped ¼ cup cocoa powder
¾ cup butter, softened

Final Touch
200 g cooking chocolate
a few dried figs
lightly sweetened whipped cream

Pears & Macaroons
in an Ocean of Chocolate

Despite the decadent title this is actually light to eat — if one stops at a small serving. Tinned or very ripe fresh pear halves are placed in a wide shallow dish and coated and surrounded with a thick chocolate custard. Cream is piped to surround each pear and the border of the chocolate custard is studded with coconut macaroons part-dipped in chocolate. Dive in. Serves 4-8 with 1 or 2 pear halves each.

Assembly
Prepare Macaroons. Peel, halve and core fresh pears. Place these or the tinned pear halves, cut side down in a single layer in a wide shallow glass dish. Pour custard to completely cover and surround pears. Either return to the refrigerator or prepare for serving as follows: place cream in piping bag using the finest plain (writing tip) nozzle and make 3 overlapping loops down the top length of the pear then with the same nozzle pipe cream in overlapping tiny spirals to completely surround border of each pear. Stud the border of the custard with a line of macaroons, chocolate side up. Serve at once with a side plate of extra macaroons.

Coconut Macaroons
This recipe makes twice as many macaroons as you'll need for this particular dessert. However they are light and easy to eat, and store well in a covered container.

Line 2 baking sheets with brown or baking paper. Lightly grease. Preheat oven to 150°C (300°F).

Beat egg whites in a large bowl until stiff. Fold in half the sugar, and ground almonds. Fold in remaining sugar, coconut, lemon peel and rum. Put mixture into a piping bag with a large plain nozzle or otherwise place tidy walnut-shaped mounds on the greased paper. Bake 20-25 minutes. Macaroons should have a golden crust but remain soft inside. Cool 1-2 minutes on a wire rack then carefully peel off cookies while still warm (once cold they tend to stick to the paper; if this happens place back in oven for 30 seconds to re-warm).

Melt chocolate in a double boiler or bowl over simmering water. Dip cooled macaroons in chocolate to coat about ⅓ of each cookie. Place on wire rack to set thoroughly before serving.

Thick Chocolate Custard
Break chocolate into a bowl over hot — not boiling — water and add milk. Heat gently until melted.

Meanwhile whisk together the egg yolks and sugar. Whisk hot chocolate into yolks. Return this to the bowl over hot water and stir constantly until thickened. Remove from heat.

Soften gelatine in cold water then stir it into the chocolate custard, making sure the gelatine is dissolved before cooling. Stand the bowl in cold water to speed cooling. Add rum. Cover and refrigerate until thick and lightly set — about 1½ hours.

Coconut Macaroons
5 egg whites
2 cups icing sugar
2 cups ground almonds
2⅔ cups coconut
grated peel of ½ lemon
1½ tbs rum
100 g cooking chocolate

Thick Chocolate Custard
150 g milk chocolate
1 cup milk
4 egg yolks
2 tbs brown sugar
2 tbs cold water
1 tsp gelatine
1 tbs dark rum
8 tinned pear halves, drained, or 4 very ripe fresh pears
1 cup lightly sweetened whipped cream

Amaretto Chocolate Cloud

For lovers of the light but luscious: a round sandwich of almond meringue layers and a chocolate amaretto cream topped with chocolate curls. It is simple to produce, few ingredients are used, but the impact (and cholesterol) is substantial. Serves 12.

Meringue
Line 3 baking trays with non-stick baking paper. Mark a 23 cm circle on each sheet. Beat egg whites until stiff, add ½ the sugar and beat until stiff and glossy. Fold in the remaining sugar. Spread the mixture evenly over the marked circles. Sprinkle with almonds. Bake 130°C (250°F) for 1 hour & 20-30 minutes until dry. Cool.

Chocolate Amaretto Cream
Melt chocolate and 3 tbs Amaretto over gentle heat in top of double boiler. Remove, add remaining Amaretto and cool. Dip each almond half-way into the chocolate, shake off excess, and place on waxed paper to harden. Whip the cream just until it begins to thicken. Add the cooled chocolate mixture and beat until thick. Sandwich the meringues with the cream and spread the remainder over the top and sides. If the mixture tends to droop down the sides (especially if the kitchen is warm) refrigerate the dessert until cold then finish applying the chocolate cream to the sides.

Chocolate Curls
Melt chocolate as before and pour onto a marble, laminated or stainless steel surface. Spread it very thinly and allow to cool completely. Using a palette knife or cleaver hold the knife at a right angle and with a sawing motion shave the chocolate to make large curls. Pick up the curls with a toothpick to prevent breakage. Place alluringly on top of the dessert. Pipe a whipped cream border around the bottom edge and stud with the chocolate-dipped almonds.

8

Meringue
6 egg whites
1 generous cup sugar
¾ cup combination fine & coarsely chopped almonds

Chocolate Amaretto Cream
225 g cooking chocolate
6 tbs Amaretto, Frangelico or coffee liqueur
600 ml cream
16 whole, well-shaped almonds

Chocolate Curls
75 g cooking chocolate

Chocolate Cookies & Cream Cake

This ingeniously constructed lightweight creation uses only six ingredients and takes but minutes to prepare. A flourless moist 'cake' is baked, reserving ¼ of the batter to later be poured on top and chilled semi-firm as the topping. Whipped cream is spread on the sides, and lightly imbedded in it — like vertical poles — at even intervals with about 15 mm between them, are (purchased) chocolate finger biscuits. More cream is piped decoratively between the cookies and in lazy swirls around the top edge of the dessert. Chill 2 hours or overnight. Serves 8-12.

Cream Cake

Place chocolate and butter in a small saucepan over low heat and stir until well combined.

Beat egg whites until foamy then gradually beat in ¼ cup of sugar until stiff peaks form.

Add ½ cup of sugar and the egg yolks to the chocolate mixture and beat at high speed for 3 minutes. Fold whites gently and thoroughly into chocolate mixture. Pour ¾ of the batter into an ungreased 20 cm springform pan. Bake at 160ºC (325ºF) for 35 minutes — cake might seem slightly 'wet'. Cool to room temperature (cake will drop while cooling).

Run a knife around the edge of the cake and remove pan sides. Pour remaining uncooked batter on top. Cover sides and garnish with cream and cookies as outlined above. Chill and serve.

Cream Cake
200 g cooking chocolate
125 g butter
¾ cup sugar
7 large eggs, separated
1¼ cup (300 ml) cream
1 packet chocolate finger biscuits

Lord of the Rings Cake

10

Those of coarse perception might call this a chocolate log but using such a name for fourteen concentric rings of chocolate cake and chocolate filling is like comparing the tales of J.R.R. Tolkien to those of Enid Blyton. How on earth does one achieve that ringed effect? Four thin cake layers are firmed under the grill, frosted, then one is snugly rolled along its short side into a compact cylinder. This is then lined up alongside the second cake layer and rolled inside it, likewise the third and fourth. The final roll will be a chunky 12 cm wide. Some remaining filling is slabbed on as rough bark and the top and sides are casually garlanded with chocolate leaves and a faint dusting of icing sugar. Tre-mendous! Serves 12.

Chocolate Cake

Line a 40 x 26 cm sponge roll tin with tinfoil. Butter this thoroughly.

Beat the egg yolks in the bowl of an electric mixer until thick and pale — about 8 minutes. Cream the butter and ¾ cup of sugar until light and fluffy. Slowly beat the yolks into the butter mixture. Add the vanilla, beating well.

In a small bowl combine the coffee, cocoa, flour and cornflour. Stir into the egg mixture by hand. Preheat the grill.

Beat the egg whites in a clean, grease-free bowl. When they form soft peaks sprinkle on the remaining ¼ cup of sugar and continue beating until they form firm but not dry peaks. Stir a large spoonful of the whites into the yolk mixture to lighten, then fold in the remaining whites.

Spread ¼ of the batter into the foil-lined and greased pan. Smooth it as gently and evenly as possible then place pan 12-14 cm under the grill. Let cook about 1-2 minutes turning the pan as necessary to make sure the entire surface is firm and lightly browned. A few light brown speckles may appear, but do not let the cake over-crisp.

Remove cake from the heat and turn over onto bench or tea-towel. Wait no more than a minute and peel tinfoil from cake. Refit foil in pan and grease again. Continue cooking the remaining three cake layers and start making the filling while they cook.

Chocolate Filling

The filling tends to dry quickly so it is made in two batches.

Place half the chocolate chips and half the butter in a double boiler or pan over hot water. Add 1 tbs water and let the chocolate melt. Stir to a smooth easily spreadable glaze adding a drop of extra water if needed. Stir in ½ tsp coffee powder or more to taste.

Spread the filling over the first cake layer, then roll it up as snugly as possible starting with the short side. You will end up with a small, compact cylinder. Place this beside your second frosted cake layer and snugly roll the cylinder inside the second layer. Continue rolling the enlarging log inside the remaining frosted cake layers.

Remove cake to serving platter. Frost the entire outside of the cake except for one end moving the spatula in rough swathes to create a bark-like effect. Cut off the unfrosted end of the cake with an angled cut to reveal the ringed pattern. Place chocolate leaves randomly on top and at sides. Dust very lightly with icing sugar.

(To make **Chocolate Leaves,** see the chapter, The Final Touch.)

Chocolate Cake
10 eggs, separated
170 g butter, softened
1 cup sugar
1 tsp vanilla
1 tsp instant coffee powder
2 tbs cocoa powder
1 cup flour
⅓ cup cornflour

Chocolate Filling
450 g chocolate morsels or chips
120 g butter
2 tbs water
1 tsp instant coffee powder

Cointreau & Chocolate Pots de Crème

Small but rich morsels. In demitasse cups or stemmed glasses you put together a layer of ricotta Cointreau mixture and a similarly laced chocolate butter cream. Garnish the side of the cup or glass with a whole slice of orange wedged securely on the lip. Take a long thin strip of orange peel and thread this through the top of the orange slice just under its border of peel and tie the strip into a jaunty knot. Serves 6.

Ricotta Mixture
225 g ricotta or cottage cheese
2 tbs icing sugar
2 tbs Cointreau or other orange liqueur
1 tbs cream
30 g finely chopped semisweet chocolate

Chocolate Buttercream
85 g semisweet chocolate
1½ tbs water

½ cup sugar
¼ cup water
¼ tsp cream of tartar

2 egg yolks
½ cup soft butter
1-2 tbs Cointreau to taste

2-3 oranges for garnish

Ricotta Mixture
Combine all ingredients well. Half-fill 6 small cups or glasses.

Chocolate Buttercream
In top of double boiler, or in a bowl set over simmering water, combine the chocolate and 1½ tbs water until the chocolate is melted. Allow it to cool without setting.

In a small saucepan combine the sugar, water and cream of tartar. Boil, brushing down the sides occasionally, until the temperature reaches 115°C (235°F) or when a drop of syrup put into a glass of cold water immediately forms a soft ball. Remove from heat.

Beat the egg yolks until light and pale. Pour the hot syrup in a thin stream into the yolks beating well. Beat the mixture until room temperature, then beat in the soft butter a tablespoon at a time until completely incorporated. Beat in the cooled chocolate and the Cointreau to taste. Chill 1 hour or longer, garnishing as above.

Chocolate Stripes

12

These fourteen layer (!) slices can be served in large dessert sections or dainty tea trolley fingers. They are composed of a rich chocolate pound cake sliced into seven layers and sandwiched with a white chocolate filling. And the whole thing is laced with Cocoribe (a rum and coconut liqueur) or tinned coconut cream. Because of refrigeration times you must make it early in the day, or a day in advance. Serves 12-16.

Assembly
Prepare cake and frosting.

If the cake has been baked in a pan with sloping sides, trim the sides of the cake to make them straight. Slice the cake horizontally with a long bread knife into seven layers (the cake when cold is firm and easy to handle). Frost each layer thickly and evenly with frosting. Place the cake in the freezer for one hour (this is a must).

Depending on whether you want dainty fingers or dessert slices, slice the cake lengthwise into 2 or 3 even sections. Then slice crosswise with 8 even cuts making a total of 16 slices or 24 fingers. Place on serving plate.

Pipe Coconut Cream Garnish in rosettes diagonally across each slice. Keep refrigerated until serving. If there is a wait longer than a couple of hours the slices will start to dry out so either slice just before serving, or slice and cover with plastic wrap, piping on cream just before serving.

Chocolate Pound Cake
This is most easily made with an electric mixer. Cream the butter until fluffy. Continue beating and add the sugar in a slow stream. Beat at high speed for 5 minutes. Slow mixer, then add vanilla. Add the eggs one at a time beating briefly after each.

Mix in dry ingredients alternately with the liquid, starting and ending with the dry. When well blended pour batter into buttered loaf pan 23cm x 12cm — preferably a pan with straight sides. Bake at 160°C in the upper third of the oven for about 50-60 minutes or until a cake tester inserted in the centre comes out clean.

Rest in pan for 20 minutes then unmould onto cake rack. Cool completely then wrap in plastic wrap or tinfoil and refrigerate several hours or overnight.

White Chocolate Frosting
Combine chocolate, sugar and cornflour in saucepan. Add boiling water and stir over low heat just until thickened. Cool briefly (placing the pan in a bowl or sink full of cold water is quickest) then stir in liqueur or coconut cream. Cool to room temperature.

Place butter in mixer and cream for 5 minutes. Gradually add chocolate mixture and beat until smooth. Chill.

Coconut Cream Garnish
Whip cream, sugar, cinnamon and Cocoribe (if there is any remaining frosting add this too) until fluffy.

Chocolate Pound Cake
1 cup softened butter
1½ cups sugar
1½ tsp vanilla
3 eggs
⅔ cup cocoa powder
rounded ¼ tsp baking powder
4 tsp coffee granules
1⅓ cup flour
½ tsp salt
¼ cup Cocoribe or tinned coconut cream
⅔ cup yoghurt

White Chocolate Frosting
250 g white chocolate, finely chopped
1 cup sugar
½ cup boiling water
1½ cups softened butter
3 tbs cornflour
¼ cup Cocoribe or coconut cream

Coconut Cream Garnish
300 ml cream
½ tsp cinnamon
2 tbs brown sugar
3 tbs Cocoribe or coconut cream

Marzipan Mardi Gras

Beckoningly colourful, of crafty design and calorific richness, this is an expensive, time consuming — though completely straightforward — piece of art. A chocolate sponge roll is filled with marzipan, sliced, bathed luxuriously in Amaretto, then used to line the bottom and sides of a springform pan. A rich chocolate filling is poured inside and allowed to set overnight. This darkly handsome dessert needs no further garnish. Serves 12.

Assembly
Prepare Cake and Ganache.

Pour liqueur into a shallow dish. Cut cake into 1 cm slices, dipping one side into liqueur. Cover the bottom of a 25 cm springform tin with some of the cake slices, dipped side down, arranging open ends of slices in the same direction. Press remaining slices around the edge of the pan to fit snugly overall. Press firmly to secure. Refrigerate briefly until the cake is chilled through. Pour filling into the cake-lined pan; cover and refrigerate overnight to set.

Cut edges of cake even with filling if necessary. Invert cake onto serving platter. Cut into small wedges with a hot knife, cleaning knife in between slices. Sit back, enjoy, and plan to miss your next meal.

Chocolate Sponge Roll
Pre-heat oven to 180°C (350°F). Line a 25 x 40 cm sponge roll tin with baking paper or parchment and butter the paper.

Beat egg yolks with sugar, salt and vanilla in electric mixer until mixture is pale yellow and forms a ribbon. Beat egg whites with cream of tartar until soft peaks form. Fold ⅓ of egg whites into egg yolk mixture to lighten, then add remaining egg whites and sifted cocoa powder. Fold in gently, spread in pan, and bake for about 25 minutes until springy. While cake is cooling, roll out marzipan between two sheets of waxed paper to form a rectangle slightly smaller than the baking pan. It must be ready when the cake comes out of the oven.

Dust a tea towel with sugar. Turn the cake out on the towel and remove paper immediately. Place marzipan on cake. Roll the cake up starting on one long side, using the towel to assist. Let the roll cool completely.

Chocolate Ganache
Bring cream to the boil and remove from heat. Sprinkle on gelatine and stir to dissolve. Place the chocolate, broken into pieces, into the cream, cover the saucepan and leave for 10 minutes. Then stir the melted chocolate thoroughly into the cream and add cut-up butter, piece by piece. Whisk until very smooth and shiny.

Chocolate Sponge Roll
- 9 eggs at room temperature, separated
- ¾ cup sugar
- pinch salt
- 1 tbs vanilla
- ¼ tsp cream of tartar
- ¾ cup cocoa powder
- 500 g marzipan or almond paste at room temperature

Chocolate Ganache
- 2 cups cream
- 2 tbs gelatine
- 600 g good quality dark chocolate
- 125 g unsalted butter
- ¾ cup Amaretto or other liqueur

Fruit Fantasies

Orange Petal Compote

A light, fruity finale to an elegant meal. Whole oranges and fine slivers of peel are soaked in spiced syrup laced with Grand Marnier. Serve the oranges in individual small bowls — the 'petals' opened slightly at the top — stripe with peel, and pour syrup over all. Either pipe whipped cream around the base of each orange or pass it round the table separately.

If you want a more substantial dessert, place circles of sponge or chiffon cake under each orange before topping as above. The cake will deliciously soak up the syrup. Serves 6.

Orange Petal Compote
Peel the oranges removing the white membrane. Slightly separate the segments into 'petals' at the top.

Slice the peel into extremely fine slivers about 4 cm (1½") long.

Pour the boiling water over the cinnamon, bay leaf, cloves; steep for five minutes and strain. Mix the strained liquid with the orange juice, honey, brown sugar and orange slivers. Boil about 10 minutes until a light syrup forms and the peel is tender. Remove from heat. Stir in the Grand Marnier and rum. Immediately pour over the oranges. Baste frequently until cool. Cover and refrigerate until thoroughly chilled or overnight.

Assemble and serve as above. There is a generous amount of peel; any extra can be stored in a covered jar in the refrigerator for several weeks and used as a topping for ice-cream, or chopped and added to cakes and other desserts.

Orange Petal Compote
6 small, firm oranges
1 cup boiling water
3 cm cinnamon stick, broken into pieces
1 crushed bay leaf
½ tsp whole cloves
½ cup orange juice
6 tbs honey
¾ cup brown sugar
1 tbs Grand Marnier
1 tbs rum

Raspberry Rainbow Mould

A shimmering, multi-layered pleasure to behold. Two layers of berry filled jelly are layered between two layers of sponge cake which have been topped with orange liqueur and marmalade, and a quick sour cream and honey filling. The individual components take only minutes preparation time, though allow six hours final setting time. Try setting this in a large bowl with a narrow base so it emerges as conically impressive as possible. Then unmould and pipe lazy ribbons of whipped cream around the two layers of cake. Serve amid gasps. Serves 8-12.

Raspberry Jelly
3 cups apple/raspberry juice or other red berry juice
1½ cups fresh or tinned raspberries or other berries
2 tbs gelatine
¼ cup Amaretto, Kirsch, Cherry Heering or more juice

Raspberry Jelly
Bring 1 cup of the juice and the gelatine to a boil; remove from heat. Stir in remaining juice and the liqueur. Place half the berries in the base of the mould and top with ⅓ of the liquid. Chill until almost set. Chill remaining jelly until almost set. Meanwhile fill the cakes.

Sour Cream Filling
250 g sour cream
250 g cream cheese
2 tbs honey
½ cup icing sugar
1 tsp vanilla

Sour Cream Filling
Place all ingredients in the blender and whizz.

Sponge Cakes
250 g (approx) sponge cake(s) equivalent to 2 cakes, each 16 cm diameter 2 cm deep
6 tbs orange liqueur or juice
¾ cup (approx) chunky, tart orange marmalade
300 ml whipped cream for garnishing

Sponge Cakes
The shape of the cakes is not too important as they can be cut to fit the mould. Slice each cake into 3 layers. Sprinkle 1 tablespoon liqueur on each of the six layers. Spread them all thinly but thoroughly with marmalade.

Once the first jelly layer is almost set, cover with one layer of cake, marmalade-side up. Pour on about ⅓ of the Sour Cream Filling and top with another cake layer, marmalade-side down. Once the remaining jelly is almost set, pour it over the cake. Top with the remaining cake and filling as before, using all the filling and cutting the cake to fit. Cover with cling wrap and chill 6 hours or longer. To unmould, dip bowl briefly in hot water and invert onto a chilled serving plate. Garnish as above.

Banana Republics

These can be as whimsical looking as their name depending on how carried away you get with their construction. There is a banana shaped meringue base topped with a chocolate cream and chocolate covered, pecan topped bananas. Instead of meringue, sponge cake may be sliced into banana shapes and used as a base. Makes 12.

Meringue

Beat egg whites, salt and cream of tartar until stiff peaks form when the beater is lifted. Gradually beat in sugar a quarter at a time until the mixture is very stiff. Fold in vanilla.

Have two baking trays covered with baking paper or greased paper. Grease corners of trays so paper will cling. Spoon or pipe meringue onto paper into 12 banana shapes. Take a good look at the size and shape of your bananas and remember that meringue will spread.

Bake at 120°C (250°F) for 1½ hours until well dried. When thoroughly cooled, store meringues in an airtight tin — they will keep if necessary for several weeks.

Topping

Whip cream with icing sugar until stiff. Stir in cocoa. Using a fluted nozzle, pipe cream onto cooled meringues. Peel bananas and cut in half lengthwise. Place a banana half on each cream-topped meringue.

Melt chocolate on top of double boiler over low heat. Pour over bananas and sprinkle with nuts before chocolate sets.

Meringue
4 egg whites
pinch of salt
½ tsp cream of tartar
1 cup caster sugar
1 tsp vanilla essence

Topping
1¼ cups cream
¼ cup icing sugar
1 tbs cocoa powder, sifted
6 small evenly coloured bananas

100 g cooking chocolate
¼ cup chopped pecans

Pawpaw & Prune Caramel Cream Pie

Might sound an unusual marriage but this is handsomely colourful and as easy as pie to prepare. The pawpaw and prunes checkerboard each other effectively, and the sour cream topping is remarkably light. The pawpaw is kept virtually raw which suits it. When pawpaw is out of season, diced banana or other raw or stewed fruit would work well. Although the pastry may be baked the day before (or baked, then frozen for several weeks) the pie should be finally assembled and eaten on the same day or the crust gets soggy. Serves 8.

Pastry
1½ cups flour
2 tbs icing sugar
¼ tsp baking powder
125 g chilled butter cut into pieces
1 egg yolk beaten with 3-4 tbs ice water

Filling
1 medium to large pawpaw, peeled and cubed
220 g pitted prunes, sliced in half
¼ cup Grand Marnier or other orange liqueur
1½ cups sour cream
2 tsp grated orange rind
1 tbs orange juice
2 tbs brown sugar
¼ cup plus 2 tbs brown sugar

Pastry
Stir flour, sugar and baking powder in bowl. Cut or rub in butter until it resembles coarse bread crumbs. Quickly stir in egg mixture to form a soft dough. Shape into a ball and wrap in plastic wrap, chilling for 30 minutes.

Roll out pastry on a floured surface to fit a greased 23 cm pie plate. Press pastry decoratively onto lip of pie pan. Prick pastry lightly with fork, line with greaseproof paper and fill with dried beans or rice (this helps prevent shrinkage with a rich pastry). Bake at 230°C (450°F) for 15 minutes then remove paper and beans. Bake for a further 5 minutes until crisp and golden. Cool to room temperature before filling.

Filling
Soak prunes overnight in liqueur.

Just before filling the pie crust, toss the prunes with the cubed pawpaw. Place in pie crust.

Combine sour cream, orange juice and rind and 2 tbs brown sugar and pour over fruit. Chill 30 minutes. Sprinkle remaining brown sugar over cream filling and leave 10-15 minutes until sugar is dissolved. Cover outer edge of pastry with foil to prevent burning and place pie under a preheated grill for about 5 minutes until bubbly brown and caramelised — watch it carefully. Serve hot (more exciting!) or cold.

Pastry Gazebo

18

Like an edible summer house for fresh fruits, this provides a memorable and somewhat flirtatious way of serving a light, seasonal finale. Despite its appearance its construction is actually simple. To serve just crack the pastry cage with a serving spoon and dish up pieces of it with the cream and berries.

Pastry Gazebo
Combine flour, sugar and salt in medium bowl. Rub, or cut in butter until mixture resembles coarse crumbs. Add water a little at a time, mixing just until moistened. Knead gently for a few strokes. Wrap and chill 30-45 minutes.

On floured surface roll out ⅓ of the pastry to 5 mm thickness. Cut into a 20 cm circle. Place on a greased baking tray. Pierce well with fork and press edges prettily. Brush lightly with egg and water glaze. Bake at 220ºC until golden brown, about 12 minutes. Cool.

Meanwhile cover the outside of an inverted 6-cup 20 cm round ovenproof bowl with foil, pressing out wrinkles. Liberally oil foil. Place on greased baking tray. Roll remaining pastry to a rectangle about 5 mm thick. From one short end cut 18 x 1 cm wide strips. Place one end of a strip at centre of the bowl, curve strip down the side to the rim. Add 8 more strips starting from the same centre top point, spacing evenly down the sides (taking care not to stretch the pastry). Drape the remaining 9 strips in opposite direction over the existing strips. Press top ends together to flatten; trim bottom ends neatly at rim.

From some of the remaining pastry shape 2 thin ropes about 46 cm long. Plait ropes together and press onto rim to form a braid all round. Press ends to seal. Cut 3-leafed strawberry leaf shapes from remaining pastry. Place at top and around rim where rope joins.

Brush all over with glaze. Bake at 220ºC until browned and crisp, 15-20 minutes. Cool completely.

Gently pull foil with basket away from the bowl, then peel foil from the basket.

Fruit & Cream Filling
Set aside 4-6 large berries for garnish. Wash and hull berries; place in bowl and sprinkle with liqueur to taste. Allow to sit 30 minutes or longer.

Just before serving, beat cream until stiff and sweeten to taste with sugar or honey. Place pastry circle on serving plate. Spoon cream in a mound on the circle, then top with drained berries. Invert pastry gazebo over the top. Decorate with reserved berries and fresh green strawberry or mint leaves. Serve at once.

Pastry
2¼ cups flour
2 tbs icing sugar
½ tsp salt
155 g butter or margarine, cut into pieces
5-7 tbs cold water

Glaze
1 egg beaten with 3 tbs water

Fruit & Cream Filling
2 punnets large, firm strawberries
1-3 tbs Cointreau or other orange flavoured liqueur
1½ cups cream
sifted icing sugar, or honey

Lemon Cream & Walnut Crisp Sandwich

This is a never-fail combination of sweet, crisp, nutty meringue — in this case, walnut — filled with a tart lemon curd and cream mixture. The Meringue is baked in a large pan, cut lengthwise in half, filled, and served in rectangular slices. The top is decorated with thick diagonal stripes of whipped cream. Serve on dessert plates and pipe a large rosette of whipped cream by one bottom corner of the slice; stud this with a thin quarter slice of lemon and a walnut half. This stores well, refrigerated overnight if necessary. Serves 8-12.

Assembly
Bake and cool Meringue. Prepare Lemon Curd and Cream Filling. Slice Meringue in half and place one half on a large flat platter or bread board. Cover with Filling, then remaining Meringue. Pipe thick diagonal ripples of whipped cream over the top, doing a double layer if necessary to use up the cream (leave enough for the rosettes though). Chill two hours or longer, before slicing with a serrated knife. Serve as outlined above.

Crisp Walnut Meringue
5 large egg whites
1 cup sugar
¼ cup cornflour
1 tsp vinegar
1¼ cups chopped walnuts

Lemon Curd and Cream Filling
175 g butter
3 large eggs
½ cup sugar
3 lemons: juice and grated peel
½ cup cream, whipped

1½ cups cream, whipped
lemon slices
walnut halves

Crisp Walnut Meringue
Beat the whites until soft peaks form. Gradually beat in the sugar until very stiff. Beat in the cornflour and vinegar. Fold in walnuts. Pour mixture into a very well buttered large roasting pan (about 30 x 35cm or two smaller rectangular pans to a similar volume: use your maths! Bake at 140°C (275°F) for 60-70 minutes until dry. Loosen with a large metal spatula to ensure that meringue doesn't stick, then allow to cool in the pan. Turn out onto the bench or a board, first cutting the meringue in half as indicated, if that is helpful. Don't worry if there is some breakage. It won't be noticed in the final assembly — use the better half as the top.

Lemon Curd and Cream Filling
Melt the butter in the top of a double boiler. Beat the eggs and sugar and add them, along with the lemon juice and peel, to the butter. Cook the mixture over a slow boil until very thick like custard, 10-15 minutes, stirring frequently. Cool, then fold in the first measure of whipped cream. Use the remainder for piping as outlined.

Hazelnut Crêpes
with Praline Ice-Cream & Chocolate Pawpaw (Papaya) Sauce

I think the title is a long enough preamble in itself. Instead of purchasing vanilla ice-cream as your basis, try any of the ice-cream recipes in this book, but keep the flavour plain so that the addition of the praline (toffee coated) hazelnuts stands out effectively. Increase the quantity of the sauce if you're a real sauce fan, and of course instead of using dried pawpaw try dried banana, candied ginger, dried pineapple or any glacé fruit. The crêpes and the ice-cream could be made weeks in advance and frozen. Serves 6.

Assembly
Prepare Ice-cream. Prepare Crêpes; these may be cooked shortly before serving and kept warm, served at room temperature, or covered with foil and reheated in a low oven. Prepare Sauce immediately before serving. Crêpes may be folded into quarters, placed on each dessert plate with a scoop of Ice-cream at the side. Swirl Sauce over one or both. Very nice served with a slice of fresh pawpaw.

Praline Ice-Cream
Allow ice-cream to slightly soften. Melt sugar in a heavy based pan over medium heat until golden brown. Remove from heat and add nuts stirring quickly. Immediately pour mixture onto a greased baking tray; cool. Chop the praline coarsely. Fold it into the softened ice-cream and return the ice-cream to the freezer until firm; one hour or longer.

Hazelnut Crêpes
Combine the flour and hazelnuts in a bowl; make a well in the centre. Beat together the eggs, oil and milk. Gradually beat into flour mixture. Cover and allow to sit one hour before using (this aerates the batter and makes for a finer crêpe).

Pour a few tablespoons of batter into a hot, greased pan. Cook briefly until brown underneath then turn and cook very briefly on the other side. As they cook lay them all out on a large surface or stack between paper sheets and towels (they stick if stacked when hot).

Chocolate Pawpaw Sauce
In a small saucepan combine all ingredients except brandy, stirring over low heat without boiling until chocolate has melted. Remove from heat and stir in brandy. Serve as outlined above accompanied with fresh pawpaw slices.

Praline Ice-Cream
1 litre vanilla ice-cream
½ cup sugar
½ cup roasted hazelnuts

Hazelnut Crêpes
½ cup flour
¼ cup ground roasted hazelnuts
3 eggs
2 tsp oil
¾ cup milk

Chocolate Pawpaw Sauce
1 tbs butter
125 g cooking chocolate
2 eggs
2 tbs brown sugar
¼ cup finely chopped dried pawpaw
½ tsp cinnamon
1-2 tbs brandy to taste

fresh pawpaw slices, optional

Banana Crêpes Créole

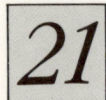

A meringue-topped crêpe gâteau, best hot but any cold left-overs are yummy too. Layers of crêpes are spread with a filling of mashed bananas, pecans and rum, then top and sides are frosted with meringue and briefly baked. Serves 8-10.

Assembly
If you choose to make the crêpes right before serving time you can top one crêpe with the Creole Filling while you cook the next. Otherwise cook the crêpes and stack between brown paper sheets. Before serving heat oven to 230ºC (450ºF). Prepare Meringue. On a heat-proof serving plate place a crêpe, top it with filling and continue until all are stacked. Frost top and sides with Meringue. Stud generously with whole pecans and bake for 3-5 minutes until browned. Serve at once.

Crêpes
¾ cup flour
3 large eggs
¾ cup water
⅔ cup milk
2 tbs melted & cooled butter
2 tsp sugar
2 tsp mixed spice

Banana Creole Filling
4 ripe bananas, mashed
¼ cup brown sugar
¾ cup chopped pecans
¼ cup rum
2 tbs lemon juice

Meringue
3 egg whites
⅓ cup sugar

Crêpes
Beat in the blender, or thoroughly by hand: first the eggs and milk, then add remaining ingredients. Cover mixture and let stand at room temperature for 1 hour or longer.

Heat 20cm (8") crêpe pan over medium heat until well heated. Oil lightly. Lade in ¼ cup batter rotating swiftly. Cook briefly, turning only once. Stack the crêpes between sheets of brown paper. If these are to be used within the day, cover the stack with a damp cloth. If they are to wait until the following day, store in a plastic bag and refrigerate. They also freeze successfully. Makes 16 crêpes.

Banana Creole Filling
Combine all ingredients.

Meringue
Beat egg whites until stiff. Gradually beat in sugar until very stiff.

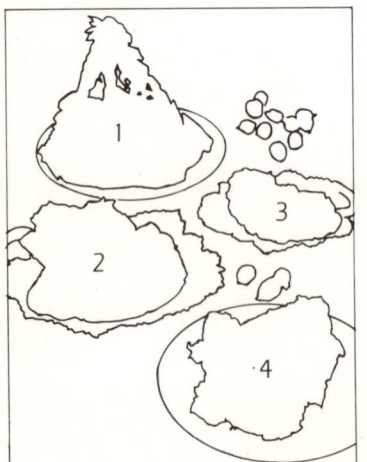

1 Pastry Gazebo (Recipe 18)
2 Crêpes Noel (Recipe 22)
3 Banana Republics (Recipe 16)
4 Raspberry Rainbow Mould (Recipe 15)

Crêpes Noël

22

For mince tart fans: a crêpe version. Crêpes are folded into triangles and filled with an apple and fruit mince filling. They are then fitted snugly, filling side up, in a round dish, looking something like a floral arrangement. Top with a one-step orange and liqueur sauce and bake briefly to warm through. Serve with vanilla ice-cream (adapt the easy recipe for homemade ice-cream; see Fig and Almond Ice-Cream). Serves 8.

Assembly
Prepare Mincemeat Filling and Orange Sauce. Fold each crêpe in half then in half again forming a triangle. Place about 3 tablespoons Filling into each crêpe — like filling an ice-cream cone. Place filled crêpes filling side up in a buttered round oven dish, fitting snugly. Cover with sauce. Bake at 200°C (400°F) for 15 minutes until heated through. Serve immediately.

Crêpes
Prepare according to Crêpes Creole recipe, making 16 crêpes.

Mincemeat Filling
Combine all ingredients.

Orange Sauce
Peel and section the oranges. Place all ingredients in a small saucepan. Simmer just to liquify the marmalade; do not boil or overcook.

Mincemeat Filling
1 cup fruit mince with brandy
1 cup coarsely chopped stewed apple (or use soaked dried apple)
½ cup chopped walnuts
2-3 tbs Cointreau or other orange liqueur to taste
3 tsp grated orange rind

Orange Sauce
2 oranges
½ cup orange marmalade
¼ cup Cointreau or other orange liqueur
1 tsp grated orange rind

1 Château Royal (Recipe 37)
2 Candied Peanut & Apricot-Filled Meringue Roll (Recipe 27)
3 Cherry Cream Gâteau (Recipe 34)
4 Peaches 'n' Cream Tipsy Torte (Recipe 26)

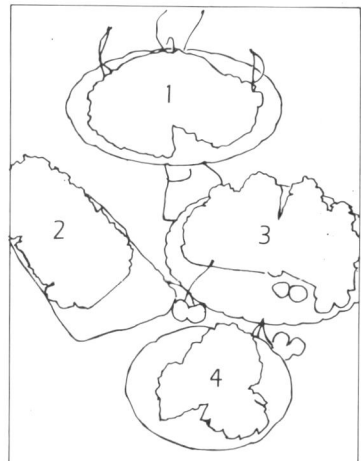

Orange Cream Mosaic

A glamorous yet delicate upside-down orange gâteau, this is composed of layers of chiffon cake, vanilla pastry cream and glazed oranges. This is an adaptation of a recipe by Gaston Lenôtre, the famous French pastry chef renowned for the freshness and lightness of his creations. Be adventurous in what shape container you choose to set this in — an oval casserole dish for instance can give a stunning effect. Serves 8.

Assembly
1¼ cups whipped cream
4-6 tbs Grand Marnier or other orange liqueur

Set aside the better looking orange slices — half the total amount — for decorating the cake. Chop the remaining ones into small pieces (reserve the syrup). Mix these with the vanilla pastry cream then fold the cream and oranges very delicately into the whipped cream.

Butter the cake pan or mould of your choice and dust with sugar. Line the mould with the orange slices, overlapping slightly. Half fill the mould with the orange pastry cream. Slice the cake into two layers and brush both layers with about 3 tbs of reserved syrup and with Grand Marnier. Place one layer of cake (or break it up to fit your mould) on top of the pastry cream. Cover with remaining pastry cream and the second cake layer. Press with a dinner plate and put a small weight on top. Refrigerate for 2 hours or longer. To turn out remove the plate and weight and dip the mould briefly into hot water. Turn out onto a serving platter. Keep refrigerated.

Glazed Oranges
Cut the oranges into very thin slices. Boil the water and sugar then add the orange slices and simmer for 2 hours. Pour the oranges and syrup into a bowl, cover, and leave until the next day.

Chiffon Cake
Make extra of these light, easy to prepare and adaptable cakes and store in the freezer for other uses.

Stir together flour, sugar and baking powder. Make a depression in the centre of the mixture and add in order: oil, egg yolks, and water. Stir until smooth.

Beat egg whites and cream of tartar until very stiff. Pour egg yolk mixture over whites and fold carefully just until blended. Pour into an ungreased 20cm springform or tube pan. Bake 160°C for 30-40 minutes or until the centre springs back when lightly touched. Immediately invert, supporting the sides of the pan on 2 up-turned small bowls so that the cake is left hanging free. Cool completely before removing from pan.

Vanilla Pastry Cream
Bring milk and vanilla to a boil. Cover and keep hot. With a whisk or electric beater beat sugar and egg yolks until the mixture whitens and forms a ribbon; then gently whisk in arrowroot.

Strain out the vanilla bean and pour the hot milk into the yolk mixture beating constantly. Pour the mixture into the saucepan, whisk in the gelatine, and boil for 1 minute whisking constantly. Pour into a bowl and lightly rub the surface of the cream with butter to keep a skin from forming as it cools.

Glazed Oranges
4 oranges
4 cups water
2¾ cups sugar

Chiffon Cake
1 cup flour
½ cup sugar
1½ tsp baking powder
¼ cup oil
3 large eggs, separated
¼ cup + 2 tbs cold water
¼ tsp cream of tartar

Vanilla Pastry Cream
1¼ cups milk
¼ vanilla bean split in half lengthwise
3 egg yolks
⅓ cup sugar
3 tbs arrowroot
2 tsp gelatine

Peach & Raspberry Cheese Tarte

Made in a springform pan with a pastry base extending part way up the sides, the pastry is topped with a peach, raspberry and ginger filling, then a subtle sour cream topping. Extra pastry is cut out into flower or other shapes and baked on top. When cool, cream can be piped lazy-river fashion in idle swirls around the top edge and between the flowers. Pipe more cream around the bottom edge of the dessert. Serves 10.

Pastry
Combine flour and salt. Cut in butter until the size of small peas. Sprinkle on peach syrup and stir until it holds together. Chill at least 2 hours. Roll out to fit bottom of 23-25cm springform pan, allowing 3 cm extra to extend up sides. Fit carefully into pan. Roll out remaining pastry and cut out 8-10 small flower shapes with a cookie cutter.

Fruit filling
Combine all ingredients except butter. Pour onto pastry. Dot with butter.

Cheese Topping
Whizz all ingredients except 2 tbs sugar in the blender. Pour onto fruit filling. Sprinkle with most of the sugar. Bake 220ºC (425ºF) for 10 min until lightly set. Place pastry flowers on top and sprinkle with sugar. Bake for 40 minutes until pastry is well browned, the centre is set and tests done when a knife is inserted. Cool and refrigerate then decorate as above.

Pastry
2 cups flour
½ tsp salt
⅔ cup butter
9 tbs peach syrup

Fruit filling
1200 g tin peach slices, drained or 3 cups fresh peach slices
2 cups fresh or frozen raspberries
½ cup sugar
3 tbs finely chopped candied ginger
½ cup peach syrup
3 tbs cornflour
2 tsp mixed spice
2 tsp vanilla
2 tbs butter

Cheese Topping
2 eggs
½ tsp nutmeg
225 g sour cream
225 g cream cheese
½ cup peach syrup
⅓ cup sugar
3 tbs cornflour
2 tbs sugar

Crème de la Crème
cream, chiffon and custard delights

Polka-Dot Pie

25

This is scrumptious. I invented this dessert for a dinner party of several overseas visitors. They all swore that they would return to New Zealand if just to get a second helping. It is not a true pie but a macaroon-like nutty base covered with a thin layer of melted chocolate, then a liqueur laced custard. Liqueur soaked prunes are arranged on top (the polka dotes) and whipped cream piped between them to cover the custard. Very simple in design and preparation but remember to make it on the day of serving; it will get soggy otherwise. Serves 8-12.

Assembly
Soak the prunes for one hour or longer in the liqueur. Meanwhile bake and cool the Nutty Crust. While baking, prepare and cool the Liqueur Custard. While the Crust is cooling melt the 120 g cooking chocolate. Place the cooled Crust on your serving platter. Cover the Crust with the chocolate, leaving a 10mm edge untouched. Let the chocolate harden.

Cover the chocolate with the cooled Custard. Arrange a row of prunes along the edge of the custard leaving a small space between them. Place another layer of prunes directly on top of the first. Heap any remaining prunes in a mound at the centre. Pipe whipped cream between the prunes and around the centre mound. Refrigerate briefly or up to several hours. Slice with a serrated knife.

Nutty Crust
Grease and flour a large baking tray and trace a 30 cm circle in the flour. Toast and then grind the nuts. In a bowl combine the nuts, cornflour, cinnamon and all but 2 tablespoons of the sugar.

Beat the egg whites until soft peaks form then gradually beat in the 2 tablespoons of sugar until stiff and glossy. Fold the nut mixture into the egg whites. Spread it evenly to cover the traced circle, leaving a small rim around the edge. Bake at 190ºC (375ºF) for 20-25 minutes then remove from the oven. Let it sit for 2-3 minutes. Slip a metal spatula underneath to ensure that it is loosened then let it continue to cool and harden on the baking tray. Once cold place it on a serving platter.

Liqueur Custard
In a small saucepan beat together the egg yolks, milk, sugar, flour and gelatine. Bring to a boil stirring constantly. Remove from heat and stir in vanilla and sour cream. Strain off any remaining liqueur from the prunes or otherwise make up ¼ cup of liqueur. Blend into custard. Chill the custard until cool. Whip the cream with the icing sugar until fluffy. Reserve half for piping later, and fold the remainder into the custard.

Soaked Prunes
1½ cups pitted prunes left whole or in halves
½ cup (approx) Cocoribe or other favourite liqueur

Nutty Crust
½ cup almonds
½ cup hazelnuts
1 tbs cornflour
1 tsp cinnamon
4 egg whites
½ cup sugar
120 g cooking chocolate for topping

Liqueur Custard
4 egg yolks
¾ cup milk
¼ cup sugar
2 tbs flour
1 tsp gelatine
1 tsp vanilla
¾ cup sour cream
1¼ cup (300ml) cream
2 tbs icing sugar
¼ cup liqueur

Peaches 'n' Cream Tipsy Torte

This looks like Rocky Road turned into a cake. It's great fun to look at and light to eat. A simple two-step fluffy white Angel Food Cake is broken into chunks, placed in a springform pan and alternated with dollops of a chocolate sauce with toasted almonds, and, a quick blender mixture of peaches and cream cheese. It sets quickly. Serves 8-12.

Assembly
Prepare and cool cake. Prepare Peaches 'n' Cream. Prepare Chocolate Nut Sauce.

On the base of a clean 25 cm springform pan place half the cake broken up into chunks about 3 cm sq. Sprinkle the cake with half the sherry. Dollop half the Chocolate Sauce on and between the cake. Pour half the Peaches 'n' Cream mixture over all. Top with the remaining cake broken likewise into chunks. Sprinkle the cake with the remaining sherry. Dollop again with sauce and peaches mixture. Using a rubber spatula flatten the top of the torte as much as possible, maintaining a decorative marbled effect. Chill two hours or longer. Remove sides of pan. Place Torte on serving plate and decorate around base with whipped cream.

Angel Food Cake
For purists I would mention that this cake isn't made in the usual manner of an Angel Food. Commonly a large measure of sugar is gradually beaten into the egg whites to make a stiff meringue. Do try this method if you want a dramatically high rising cake. A denser, shorter version is more suited to this torte.

In a small bowl combine flour and ¾ cup sugar. In a large bowl beat egg whites with cream of tartar until foamy. Sprinkle in the 2 tablespoons of sugar and beat until stiff peaks form. Sprinkle flavourings on and carefully fold in flour mixture ⅓ at a time until completely incorporated. Pour batter into an ungreased 20-23 cm tube pan or springform pan. Bake at 190ºC (375ºF) for 25-30 minutes until the top springs back when lightly touched. Remove from the oven and invert onto a wire rack. Let hang upside down until cake is completely cool. Remove from pan.

Peaches 'n' Cream
Strain the syrup from the peaches and reserve. In a small saucepan heat ½ cup of syrup until simmering. Remove from heat and whisk in 1 tablespoon gelatine until dissolved. Set aside.

In a blender or food processor whizz cream cheese, honey, remaining peach syrup and 1½ cups peach slices. Slice remaining peach slices into small to medium chunks. In a bowl combine the peach chunks, cream cheese mixture and gelatine. Chill until slightly thickened about 15 minutes.

Chocolate Nut Sauce
Melt about one third of the butter over medium heat. Coarsely chop the almonds and toast in the butter until medium brown. Remove from the heat. Stir in remaining butter and chocolate. Once the chocolate has melted stir in the ¼ cup cream.

Whip the remaining cream with the icing sugar until fluffy. Use to decorate the outer edge of the finished dessert.

Angel Food Cake
1 cup flour
¾ cup sugar
2 tbs sugar
1½ cups egg whites (8-12)
1½ tsp cream of tartar
¼ tsp salt
1 tsp vanilla
½ tsp almond essence

Peaches 'n' Cream
820 g tin peach slices
250 g cream cheese
¼ cup honey
1 tbs gelatine
6-8 tbs sherry to taste

Chocolate Nut Sauce
50 g butter
¾ cup almonds
150 g chocolate
¼ cup cream

1 cup cream
3 tbs icing sugar

Candied Peanut & Apricot-Filled Meringue Roll

27

A sort of hybrid sponge roll and pavlova. The meringue is baked in a large sheet, cooled and covered with whipped cream, soaked dried apricots and crunchy peanut candy, rolled and sliced. Not too sweet, easy to prepare and eat! Makes twelve slices but remember the lightness of this dessert: many diners might want two pieces. (The recipe is easily halved — bake in a sponge roll tin for 18-20 minutes.) Serves 6-12.

Filling

180 g dried apricots
1 cup boiling water
200 g peanut brittle or sugared or Viennese-style nuts
40 g peanut candy as above, chopped and reserved for garnish
600 ml cream whipped with:
  8 tbs icing sugar
  2 tsp vanilla
(reserve ½ cup whipped cream for garnishing)

Meringue

10 egg whites
5 tbs vinegar
2½ tbs cornflour
15 tbs sugar
5 tbs extra sugar
½ cup or more coconut

Filling

Dice apricots, soak in boiling water (adding more if necessary to cover) and leave overnight. Drain off any excess water after soaking. Combine apricots and the 200 g chopped peanut brittle.

Meringue

Line a large pan (approximately 32 cm x 35 cm) with non-stick waxed paper or tinfoil and grease generously. A flat baking tray may be used, if you use tinfoil and build up secure sides with it.

Beat egg whites until stiff then beat in vinegar and cornflour. Gradually add the 15 tbs sugar and beat until stiff. Beat well for 10 minutes. Fold in the remaining 5 tbs sugar.

Pour mixture into lined pan. Sprinkle generously with coconut. Bake for 25 minutes at 180°C (350°F).

Turn meringue out onto a tea towel coconut side down and cool. When meringue is just cool but still pliable spread with the whipped cream, apricots and nuts. Roll immediately from one long side to the next as for a sponge roll. Place on serving plate. Pipe top with diagonal ripples of whipped cream and stud the ripples generously with the reserved peanut candy. Chill in refrigerator for one to six hours to set.

Orange & Chocolate Profiteroles

A variation on the classic. Profiteroles are tiny choux buns (like round éclairs), purchased or home-made — and they're easy to make. In this case they are filled with an Orange Pastry Cream, piled in a rough pyramid on a serving platter and covered with a trail of Chocolate Grand Marnier Sauce. Sprinkle with flaked almonds. Guests love the opulent profusion of the presentation and can prise or topple several gooey buns for themselves. Serves 8-10.

Assembly
Prepare and cool Choux Buns. Prepare and chill Orange Pastry Cream. No more than two hours before serving prepare Chocolate Grand Marnier Sauce. Slice each bun almost in half horizontally. Fill with Cream mounding it more on the cut side of the bun, so that it is generously visible. Stack on a serving platter in a rough pyramid and as you stack dollop Sauce over each. When stacked sprinkle with flaked almonds.

Choux Buns
These freeze well unfilled.

In a medium saucepan over high heat bring to the boil the water, butter and salt. Remove from heat. Immediately add the flour all at once. With a wooden spoon vigorously stir the mixture until it will leave the side of the pan and form a ball. Add the eggs, one at a time, beating well after each.

Place tidy tablespoons of the mixture at regular intervals on two greased baking trays to make 40 choux buns. Bake at 190°C (375°F) for 30-35 minutes until golden. Remove to racks to cool.

Orange Pastry Cream
In a medium saucepan combine milk, orange juice, sugar, egg yolks, flour and gelatine. Bring to a rolling boil, then remove from heat. Stir in the orange peel, Grand Marnier and vanilla. Chill, covered, until cold, 20-30 minutes. Beat cream until soft peaks form, fold into custard.

Chocolate Grand Marnier Sauce
Bring cream to a boil; remove from heat and stir in broken chocolate pieces until melted. Stir in liqueur. Use the flaked almonds as outlined for a garnish.

Choux Buns
1 cup water
½ cup butter
pinch salt
1 cup flour
4 large eggs

Orange Pastry Cream
1½ cups milk
juice of two large oranges — about 1 cup
4 large egg yolks
½ cup sugar
4 tbs flour
2 tsp gelatine
grated rind of 1½ large oranges
3 tbs Grand Marnier or other orange liqueur
1 tsp vanilla
1 cup cream

Chocolate Grand Marnier Sauce
130 g cooking chocolate
5 tbs cream
3 tbs Grand Marnier or other orange liqueur
flaked almonds

Coffee Velvet

29

A fluffy coffee torte perhaps decadent of appearance but divinely light in taste. There is an almond macaroon base, a liqueur soaked prune and cream stripe, topped with coffee chiffon. Decorate with piped whipped cream around the top edge and filigree chocolate (simply melt 2 tbs chocolate and drizzle randomly and decoratively from the tip of a spoon). Serves 8-10.

Base
1½ cups crushed almond macaroons (or use coconut macaroons & add 1 tsp almond essence)
2 tbs brown sugar
6 tbs softened butter or margarine

Prune Liqueur Filling
2 cup diced pitted prunes
3 tbs Kahlua, Frangelico or Amaretto
300 ml cream

Coffee Chiffon
2 cups water
1 cup milk
2 tbs gelatine
4 eggs, separated
2 tbs instant coffee
¾ cup packed brown sugar

Base
Ingredients may all be blended right in the 23 cm springform pan. Press mixture onto base and part way up sides. Bake at 180°C for 8 minutes until lightly browned. Cool. Top with Liqueur Prune Filling then the Coffee Chiffon. Chill 2 hours or longer until set.

Prune Liqueur Filling
Soak prunes in liqueur at least one hour. Whip cream and fold in prunes and liqueur.

Coffee Chiffon
In a large saucepan whisk water, milk, gelatine, egg yolks, coffee and sugar. Over medium heat, stirring constantly, cook until lightly thickened about 15-20 minutes. Do not boil or the coffee will taste bitter. Refrigerate until mixture mounds when dropped from a spoon, about 50 minutes.

Beat egg whites until stiff. Beat coffee mixture with same electric beaters at high speed until fluffy. Fold whites into coffee mixture.

Streusel-Topped Poppyseed Cheesecake

A German-style cheesecake. A plain, dense filling on a pastry base, topped with a lemon, poppyseed mixture and a crisp brown sugar streusel. Despite its several components, it is simple to produce with each element exquisitely complementing the other. Serves 10-12.

Assembly
Prepare and part-bake the pastry. Top with the cheese filling and bake. Cover with Lemon Poppyseed Topping. Sprinkle on Streusel Topping in a spoke fashion leaving some dark poppyseed mixture showing through. Place briefly under the grill until brown and bubbly. Remove pan sides and place cake on serving plate. Chill thoroughly for 2 hours or longer. Serve.

Pastry Base
Place flour in a mixing bowl. Cut in the butter until the size of small peas. Lightly beat the egg. Stir the sugar into the flour, then the egg. Knead lightly until a soft dough forms. Roll out pastry on a lightly floured surface until slightly larger than a 20 cm circle. Press lightly onto the base of a 20 cm springform pan, forming a small rim. Bake at 180°C (350°F) for 10-15 minutes until lightly coloured.

Cheesecake Filling
Whizz in a blender or food processor the cream cheese and sour cream or yoghurt until smooth. Add the sugar and whizz until the sugar is dissolved. Whizz in eggs and vanilla. Pour onto the pastry base and bake for 20 minutes until just firm. Turn off heat and leave in the oven for 1½ hours.

Lemon Poppyseed Filling
Place all the ingredients in a small saucepan and bring to a boil; simmer for 5 minutes until thick and tender. Spread on top of the cheesecake after its full baking time.

Streusel Topping
Place the flour in a mixing bowl and cut in butter until it resembles coarse breadcrumbs. Stir in the sugar. Use on top of the poppyseed mixture as indicated.

Pastry Base
1 cup flour
60 g butter
1 tbs sugar
1 large egg

Cheesecake Filling
375 g cream cheese, softened
¼ cup sour cream or yoghurt
½ cup sugar
2 large eggs
1 tsp vanilla

Lemon Poppyseed Filling
½ cup poppyseeds
1 cup raisins
½ cup milk
grated peel and juice of 1 large lemon
½ tsp vanilla

Streusel Topping
⅓ cup flour
60 g butter
⅓ cup brown sugar

Rich, Creamy Italian Cheesecake

31

A baked continental style cheesecake as comparable to the standard pallid New Zealand cheesecake as the Colosseum is to Eden Park. When the cake is completed arrange twists of lemon, pieces of candied ginger and citrus leaves as for a floral decoration around the base. Serve cold or at room temperature. Serves 12.

Shortcrust Pastry
1 heaped cup flour
4 tbs cold water
125 g cold butter
pinch salt

Cheesecake Filling
6 eggs separated
½ cup flour
1 cup sultanas or fruit cake mix
grated rind and juice of
  1 large lemon
300 ml cream
500 g ricotta cheese
250 g softened cream cheese
150 g sour cream
2 tbs finely chopped candied
  ginger (optional)

Shortcrust Pastry
Cut butter into flour with pastry blender or 2 dull knives (or prepare as directed in food processor) until butter is well covered with flour. Blend with fingers until butter is the size of coarse bread crumbs. Make a well in the centre and add 3 tbs cold water. Stir, then knead lightly to make a smooth dough. Roll out to fit a 23 cm springform pan base plus 15 mm up the sides. Fit into the pan without stretching and refrigerate until chilled. Bake 200ºC 8-10 minutes until lightly browned.

Cheesecake Filling
Beat the egg yolks, flour and sugar until creamy. Beat in cream and sour cream. In separate bowl beat cream cheese, ricotta, lemon rind and juice. Beat into yolk mixture, add candied ginger and pour into baked crust. Bake 170ºC for 1¾ hours until a skewer inserted in the centre tests dry and centre jiggles firmly rather than "wetly".

Cool thoroughly in tin away from draughts. Remove pan sides, place on serving plate and dredge top with icing sugar.

Irish Cream Pie

Light and luscious to eat but with a subtly provocative flavour. There is a crunchy chocolate crust and a mousse-like filling enhanced by the addition of Baileys Irish Cream, and a Mocha Cream Topping. Another good do-ahead dessert. Serves 8.

Chocolate Crust
Finely chop cookies. Mix with remaining ingredients. Press onto base and part-way up sides of 20-23 cm springform pan. Refrigerate while preparing filling.

Filling
Beat cream cheese, honey and sugar until smooth. Add egg yolks one at a time beating well after each. Add the Irish Cream and beat well. Sprinkle gelatine over 2½ tbs water. Stand the bowl in hot water to dissolve gelatine. Cool, add to cream cheese mixture, beat until well combined.

Beat ½ cup cream to soft peaks, fold into cream cheese mixture.

Beat egg whites until soft peaks form. Fold into cream mixture. Pour into pie crust. Chill several hours or until set. Decorate border of pie with piped Mocha Cream; sprinkle with cinnamon. Chill and serve.

Mocha Cream
Dissolve coffee and cinnamon in hot water. Combine with cocoa and 1½ cups cream and beat until peaks form.

Chocolate Crust
200 g chocolate and toffee covered cookies (such as Toffee Pops)
½ cup coconut
½ tsp cinnamon
60 g butter, melted

Filling
125 g softened cream cheese
2 eggs, separated
2 tsp gelatine
½ cup cream
1 tbs honey
1 tbs sugar
½ cup Baileys Irish Cream
2½ tbs water

Mocha Cream
1 tbs cocoa powder
2 tsp instant coffee granules
1 tbs hot water
¼ tsp cinnamon
1½ cups cream
cinnamon for sprinkling

Mixed Fruit & Pecan Tarte

33

Sometimes you feel like making (and eating) something as prosaic and eternally popular as apple pie. Even this old standby can be transformed into a glamour girl with a few deft touches. Baking it in a springform pan so it emerges impressively free-standing is one such touch, as is the addition of never-fail flaky pastry, bananas, orange marmalade and a crunchy pecan topping. Serve warm or at room temperature — too hot and it will crumble when slicing — with whipped cream or ice-cream. Serves 8.

Pastry
2 cups flour
125 g butter
1 large egg
2 tbs cold water

Mixed Fruit Filling
5 large apples
2 tbs butter
¼ cup brown sugar
¼ cup marmalade
1 tsp cinnamon
3 large bananas, diced

¾ cup chopped pecans
⅓ cup brown sugar
1 tsp cinnamon
few tbs butter

Pastry
Rub or cut butter into flour. Beat the egg and water together. Mix into flour to form a soft dough, kneading lightly. Chill at least 30 minutes before using — this helps make the pastry flaky.

Roll out dough to fit a 20 cm springform pan, extending dough about 5 cm up the sides. Press top edge with a fork to decorate.

Mixed Fruit Filling
Peel, core and thickly slice apples. Melt the 2 tablespoons of butter in a small saucepan and stir in apples, cinnamon and marmalade. Sprinkle on the ¼ cup sugar, cover with a lid, and let fruit steam, undisturbed, for about 5 minutes until just soft. Stir in the chopped banana and pour mixture into the pastry lined pan.

Combine the nuts, sugar and cinnamon and use this to cover the fruit. Dot generously with butter. Bake at 200°C (400°F) for 25 minutes until cooked and golden brown. Cool 15 minutes or longer then remove pan sides. Cool to desired temperature, place on serving plate and serve.

Cherry Cream Gâteau

34

A pretty dessert with a satiny marbled pink glaze. Three rounds of flaky pastry are baken then layered with cherries in syrup and a toasted coconut whipped cream. All very simple really. The top pastry round is covered with red jelly then a light lemon glaze which creates the shimmery marbled effect. Decorate the top outer edge with rosettes of cream topped with a candied or fresh cherry on a stem. Makes 12 light to eat slices — some people may want two.

Assembly
Place one pastry round on a serving plate. Surround the edge of the pastry with a wall of Coconut Cream. Keeping inside the cream barrier, top the pastry with the Cherry Filling. Cover lightly with Coconut Cream. Top with second pastry round. Cover the top and sides of the gâteau with the remaining Coconut Cream. Top with glazed pastry slices. Decorate each with a cream rosette and top with a cherry. Chill at least four hours or overnight (this needs to be cold and firm to slice well). Use a serrated knife for slicing.

Cherry and Coconut Cream Fillings and Marbled Topping
Sprinkle two baking sheets with cold water. Cut or roll out pastry to three 20 cm (8") round. Place on baking sheets and refrigerate for 15 minutes. Bake at 200ºC (400ºF) for 12-15 minutes until lightly browned. Cool on racks, piercing the pastry tops with a sharp knife to help them deflate. Press rounds gently so that they are no higher than 10 mm (½").

Warm the jelly over low heat until just liquified. Spread over the thinnest, most even pastry board (flip one over onto its smooth bottom surface). Combine ¾ cup icing sugar and lemon juice to make a glaze. Spread lightly over the jelly so that the pink shows through (this will intensify with cooling). Allow to set. Cut with a sharp knife into 12 slices. This must be done before final assembly; if you try to otherwise slice the gâteau the cream filling will ooze out.

Drain the cherries, placing the juice in a small saucepan. Combine the juice with the cinnamon and cornflour. Bring to a boil stirring constantly until thick. Remove from heat. Stir in cherries. Cool completely until very thick.

Whip the cream and the 5 tbs icing sugar until thick. Place about 6 tbs of cream in a piping bag with a fluted nozzle. Stir the toasted coconut into the remaining cream.

Cherry and Coconut Cream Fillings and Marbled Topping
350-400 g frozen puff pastry, thawed
3 tbs red currant or other red jelly
¾ cup icing sugar
4 tsp lemon juice
450 g tin pitted dark cherries in syrup
½ tsp cinnamon
2 tbs cornflour
2½ cups (600 ml) cream
5 tbs icing sugar
1 cup toasted coconut
12 candied or fresh cherries

Three-Coloured Lady

35

This attractive dessert is lined with lady-fingers and named for its three fillings of vanilla and toasted coconut, puréed apricots, and caramel. It will unmould leaving a bald spot at the top which can be decorated lavishly with whipped cream and sliced apricots or toasted coconut. Pipe cream rosettes around the base and stud alternately with dried apricots cut in half. This is surprisingly quick to prepare and being in fact just a dressed-up custard has the talent of appealing to both adults and children. Experiment with a variety of contrasting fillings like chocolate and banana or strawberry and lemon. Use the left-over egg whites to make Amaretto Chocolate Cloud. Serves 12.

Vanilla cream

2 cups milk
¼ cup sugar
2 tbs cornflour
3 lightly beaten egg yolks
4 tsp gelatine
2 tsp vanilla
2 tbs butter
¾ cup toasted large flaked coconut
300 ml cream

Apricot Purée

1 cup dried apricots
1¼ cups water
2 tbs apricot brandy or Baileys Irish Cream (optional)

Caramel Cream

2½ cups milk
½ cup brown sugar
3 tbs cornflour
3 lightly beaten egg yolks
1 tsp cinnamon
4 tsp gelatine
1 tsp instant coffee granules
2 tsp Milo
2 tbs butter
1 tsp vanilla
300 ml cream

Assembly

16-20 lady-fingers
few tsp soft butter

Lightly butter the sides of a ribbed brioche mould (22 cm) or charlotte mould (16 cm). Better too big than too small. Fit in lady fingers snugly side by side. If they do not stand without assistance put a tiny drop of butter at their top end to act as glue against the bowl. Fill the mould half-way with the vanilla cream. Chill until fairly set. Top with apricot purée; cover with the caramel cream and refrigerate for 2-3 hours.

To turn out dip mould briefly in hot water and invert onto a platter. Decorate as outlined above.

Vanilla cream

Bring to a boil over medium heat the milk, sugar, yolks, cornflour and gelatine. Stir constantly. Boil 1 minute then remove from heat. Add butter, vanilla and coconut. To cool, quickly place pot in a sink full of cold water. Beat cream until fluffy and when custard is cool fold in the cream.

Apricot Purée

Bring ingredients to a boil (minus the liqueur if used; this can be added after cooking) and simmer for 15 minutes. Cool somewhat and purée in the blender.

Caramel Cream

Bring to a boil over medium heat the milk, sugar, cornflour, yolks, gelatine and cinnamon. Stir constantly. Boil 1 minute. Remove from heat and add butter, vanilla, coffee and Milo. Cool as for vanilla cream. Fold in cream.

Fantasy Islands

36

Set in a shallow dish or bowl, a silky coffee and ginger (the latter is optional) custard supports a chain of crisp meringue 'islands'. Whipped cream is piped in foamy waves between them and sprinkled with a blend of fine coffee granules and cinnamon. The bite of coffee and ginger, the combination of smooth and moist, dry and crisp is very pleasing. Serves 4.

Meringues
Make ½ the Meringue recipe (see Banana Republics) piped into small spirals. There will be some left over which are nice served on the side, or make the full recipe. Meringues will keep for several weeks when stored in an airtight container.

Coffee and Ginger Custard
Measure coffee into a small saucepan and add boiling water. Over medium heat add milk, stirring now and then until almost boiling (do not boil or coffee will taste bitter).

Meanwhile whisk together egg yolks and sugar. Pour hot milk onto yolks, whisking well. Return this to the saucepan over low-medium heat and stir constantly with a wooden spoon until slightly thickened. Remove from heat.

Soften gelatine in the cold water then stir this into the coffee mixture until gelatine is all dissolved. Add the ginger. Cool slightly then add the vanilla or whiskey and pour into a wide, shallow glass dish or bowl. Refrigerate until set.

Arrange small meringues all over the top. Pipe the whipped cream in between so only the tips of the meringues show. Sprinkle the cream with Coffee Cinnamon Topping. Refrigerate or serve right away.

Coffee Cinnamon Topping
Stir to combine. (Make extra and use to top after-dinner coffees.)

Coffee and Ginger Custard
1 tbs instant coffee granules
2 tbs boiling water
1⅓ cups milk
3 egg yolks
2 tbs brown sugar
2 tbs cold water
1¼ tsp gelatine
1 tsp vanilla or 1 tbs whiskey
2-3 tsp drained, finely chopped ginger in syrup

Coffee Cinnamon Topping
1½ tsp instant coffee granules
1 tsp packed brown sugar
¼ tsp cinnamon

Château Royal

37

A visually stunning yet simple to prepare and light to eat concoction. There is a subtly distinctive white wine custard surrounded by a helmet of lemon-filled sponge roll slices. If you're really pressed for time buy the sponge roll and the lemon curd and preparation time is only minutes. Serves 10-12.

Sponge Roll
Line a 33 x 23 cm cake pan with waxed paper and grease it well. Beat 6 egg yolks with ½ the sugar until pale and creamy, 5-10 minutes with the electric mixer. Beat egg whites until frothy, slowly sprinkle in remaining sugar and continue to beat until very stiff. Drop the whites onto the yolks. Sprinkle flour onto whites and with a metal spoon fold in carefully but thoroughly. Spread evenly in prepared pan. Bake 220°C (425°F) for 10-12 minutes until toothpick inserted in centre comes out clean.

Place a sheet of waxed paper on a damp cloth. Sprinkle the paper with sugar. Turn the cake onto the paper. Strip off the waxed paper and trim the edges of the cake. Fill with jam and roll up tightly from the long side. Let cool.

Cut cooled roll into 18 slices. Line a 1.5 L (6¼ cup) bowl with 14 slices pressing well against each other to cover bottom and sides of bowl.

White Wine Filling
In saucepan simmer wine, sugar and gelatine until sugar is dissolved. Cool until almost set, then beat in lemon rind and juice and lemon curd. Whip cream; reserve ¼ of it for garnishing. Fold cream into wine custard. Pour into cake-lined bowl; cover carefully with remaining sponge roll slices. Chill until set about 1 hour or overnight.

Turn out onto serving plate. Pipe rosettes of cream around the edge and stud with whole fresh cherries.

Lemon Curd
In top of double boiler, combine all ingredients. Mix well. Set over boiling water, stirring constantly with a wooden spoon for 10-15 minutes or until mixture is thick and smooth.

NOTE: Why not double the recipe and use the lemon curd as a toast spread, cake or cookie filling?

A double boiler can be improvised by using a standard two-saucepan steamer unit. Place a small metal bowl in the top perforated pot and simmer water in the bottom pot.

Sponge Roll
4 eggs plus 2 egg yolks
½ cup sugar
½ tsp vanilla
¾ cup flour
¼ cup cornflour
500 g cherry or raspberry jam mixed with 2 tbs sherry

White Wine Filling
2 tbs gelatine
1 cup white wine
½ cup sugar
juice & rind of 1 lemon
¾ cup lemon curd
300 ml cream
12 fresh cherries (keep stems on) or tinned

Lemon Curd
¼ cup butter
¼ cup honey
2 tbs lemon peel
¼ cup lemon juice
3 large eggs, lightly beaten

Stilton Mousse

I served this at our mini colonial salute to the Royal Wedding. It is light but distinctive, a fluffy 'feminine' variation on an after dinner cheese board. Basically a white sauce is flavoured with crumbled Stilton (blue cheese or a runny brie work well too) and whipped cream and set in a souffle dish or individual ramekins. Top with finely chopped parsley and pipe unsweetened whipped cream around the edge. Serve with English flaky-pastry crackers and fresh green grapes. This would also make a more-ish first course or luncheon dish. Serves 8-12.

Stilton Mousse
Melt the butter and blend in the flour. Gradually blend in the milk. Whisk in the egg yolks and the nutmeg, then whisk in the gelatine. Bring to a boil and simmer for 3 minutes. Remove from the heat and crumble in the Stilton; stir in the spring onions. Stir in the wine and salt and pepper to taste. Cool until thick but not set. Beat the cream until stiff; beat the egg whites until stiff. Fold the cream into the cheese mixture, then fold in the egg whites. Pour into a 5-6 cup decorative casserole dish. Cover the top with finely chopped parsley. Pipe whipped cream around the edge. Chill until set, 3 hours or more.

Stilton Mousse
2 tbs butter
4 tbs flour
1½ cups milk
3 large eggs, separated
¼ tsp nutmeg
1 tbs gelatine
230 g Stilton
3 spring onions, diced
¾ cup dry white wine
salt & pepper
¾ cup cream
chopped parsley
extra whipped cream for piping

From the Tea Trolley
elegant cakes and pastries

Honeyed Hedgehog

39

A light toasted almond cake of rough good looks, faintly dabbled with an Amaretto syrup, then covered with a chocolate glaze and coarse chunks of chocolate honey comb.

Assembly
3 chocolate coated 'honeycomb' bars (such as Crunchy bars) coarsely chopped

Slice cake in half horizontally. Drizzle both cut faces with hot Syrup. Place bottom layer on serving plate and cover with Chocolate Glaze. Top with other cake layer and cover cake completely with Glaze. While Glaze is still tacky, sprinkle top and sides with chopped chocolate bars.

Toasted Almond Cake
Place eggs, yolks and sugar in the metal bowl of an electric mixer. Place bowl over low heat and whisk until well warmed and sugar is dissolved (or use a glass bowl and place over hot water). Place bowl on machine and beat for 10 minutes. Eggs should be very thick and form a heavy ribbon when beaters are raised.

Add the almonds and essences and beat briefly. Fold in flour working rapidly and gently. Carefully fold in butter.

Pour into greased and floured 23 cm tube or bundt pan. Bake at 180°C for 30-35 minutes until the cake shrinks slightly from the sides of the pan and the centre tests dry when a skewer is inserted. Let cool for 10 minutes then unmould onto a rack. Cool completely.

Amaretto Syrup
Bring the sugar and water to a boil and simmer briskly for 3 minutes. Cool briefly and add Amaretto.

Chocolate Glaze
Bring to a boil the chocolate, water, sugar and arrowroot. Cook at a slow boil, stirring constantly, for 3 minutes. Off the heat stir in butter 1 tbs at a time, then add vanilla and icing sugar. Cool until of good spreading consistency.

Toasted Almond Cake
6 eggs plus 2 egg yolks
½ cup packed brown sugar
1 cup ground, toasted almonds
1 tsp vanilla
½ tsp almond essence
1 cup flour
3 tbs butter, melted & browned

Amaretto Syrup
⅓ cup sugar
½ cup water
2 tbs Amaretto

Chocolate Glaze
115 g cooking chocolate
½ cup brown sugar
½ cup hot water
1 tbs arrowroot
5 tbs butter
1 tsp vanilla
5 tbs icing sugar

Butter Berry Teacake

40

This has a pastry base, a buttery cake main filling, topped with a boysenberry (or other berry) stripe and a nut meringue. Might sound exhausting, but is surprisingly straightforward to produce. The external appearance is a trifle brown so garnish the base with piped whipped cream and whole berries. Or serve it already sliced; cut, it is delightfully marbled and intriguing. Remember the nut meringue as an interesting topping for other cakes, pies, bars and cookies. Make extra pastry and freeze it in lots for other desserts like Rich Creamy Italian Cheesecake. Serves 10-12.

Pastry
Cream butter and sugar. Stir in flour. Knead well adding enough ice water to make a soft dough. Chill at least one hour. Roll out to fit base plus slightly up sides of 23 cm springform pan. Fit into pan and prick with fork. Bake 220°C (425°F) for 15-18 minutes until golden. Remove from oven. Reduce heat to 190°C (375°F).

Cake
Beat butter, ½ the sugar, egg yolks and lemon peel until pale and fluffy. Beat egg whites until stiff then fold in remaining sugar. Carefully fold whites into yolks. Mixture may be streaky but will blend further later. Fold in flour and cornflour. Pour batter over pastry, top with berries. If berries have a lot of juice add 1 tbs cornflour or arrowroot. Bake 70 minutes until lightly done.

Nut Meringue
Beat egg whites until frothy. Gradually beat in sugar until stiff and glossy. Fold in nuts. Increase heat to 200°C (400°F). Top with Nut Meringue and bake for 15 minutes. Cool 15 minutes then remove sides and cool completely.

Pastry
8 tbs soft butter
¼ cup sugar
1½ cups flour
2-3 tbs ice water

Cake
300 g very soft butter
1¼ cups sugar
6 eggs, separated
2 tsp grated lemon peel
1¼ cups flour
1¼ cups cornflour
2 cups fresh, frozen or tinned & drained boysenberries or other berries

Nut Meringue
2 egg whites
½ cup sugar
1 cup ground almonds or walnuts

Viennese Ribbon Cake

41

A pretty pink exterior of mock fondant coats a cake of three layers: two light Viennese sponge layers surrounding a dark, moist mystery layer. This layer is simply one layer of sponge which has been cubed and coated with a rum, orange and chocolate syrup, and sandwiched back between the two cake layers. Straightforward to make, exotic to eat and look at. There is one catch though — it's formed over a three-day period! One day, make the cake. Wait until the next day (or up to three days, or freeze the cake) to let it dry out somewhat so it will be more absorbant for the middle layer later. Then cube, coat and sandwich in the middle layer and weight the reassembled cake with a 1-1½ kg object (chopping board, books etc.) to cover it completely, and let it sit overnight or longer. Frost and serve.

Assembly

Day One — Bake, cool and store cake.

Day Two — Prepare Syrup. Slice cake into 3 even layers. Slice the middle layer into 5mm (¼") dice. Toss the cubes with the syrup, adding more orange juice if necessary so it is thoroughly moist but not dripping. Place the bottom cake layer on a serving plate. Pack the cake mixture on top, smooth, and cover with top cake layer. Cover cake with plastic wrap or place inside a plastic bag. Cover with weight as outlined earlier. Leave overnight or longer.

Day Three — Frost as follows: pour 'fondant' onto top of cake; smooth over top and down sides. Run an icing comb (or clean, wide-toothed hair comb) lightly over top in zigzag fashion to make wriggly lines all over top of cake. Leave sides smooth. Allow to set briefly until firm (on a hot day place in refrigerator for 10 minutes to firm). Serve.

Viennese Sponge Cake

Another delicious though completely different use of this basic cake; see also the Strauss Waltz Cake and Zabaglione Sponge Cake recipes.

Separate eggs while cold (they're easier to separate then), putting the whites into a large bowl and the yolks into a small bowl. Allow them to sit at least 30 minutes until at room temperature (warm eggs beat up fluffier).

Beat the egg whites until soft peaks form, then gradually beat in ½ the ¾ cup sugar until a very stiff meringue forms.

Beat the egg yolks with the remaining sugar and vanilla until light, pale and doubled in volume. Fold ¼ of the whites into the yolks to lighten the mixture. Fold in the remaining whites. Fold in flour, salt and peel.

Pour into a buttered and floured 20 cm (8") springform pan. Bake at 180ºC (350ºF) for 40-50 minutes. To test, prod the centre of the cake firmly but gently: as soon as it springs back (however hesitantly!) remove it from the oven. Do not overbake.

Dust the top of the cake lightly with flour. Immediately overturn onto a warm plate. If the pan comes loose easily, remove it, if not let it sit there until the cake is completely cool. Once cool, store in a plastic bag or container for a day or longer.

Rum, Orange and Chocolate Syrup

Melt chocolate, butter and marmalade over low heat until just melted. Stir in rum and orange juice and heat until just simmering. Do not boil.

Pink Raspberry 'Fondant'

Place butter and jam in small saucepan and over low heat cook gently until butter is melted. Remove from heat. Stir in icing sugar until thick, but easy to spread and a bit thinner than a usual frosting.

Viennese Sponge Cake
6 large eggs
¾ cup sugar
1 tsp vanilla
1 cup flour
dash salt
grated peel of ½ lemon

Rum, Orange and Chocolate Syrup
200 g cooking chocolate
3 tbs butter
2 tbs orange marmalade
⅓-½ cup orange juice
¼ cup rum

Pink Raspberry 'Fondant'
⅓ cup butter
3 tbs raspberry jam
1-1¼ cups icing sugar

Nut-topped, Rum-drenched, Banana Pound Cake

Another rich one but special served in small slices with coffee. Very simple to prepare for the grandeur of its final statement. Prepare it the day before serving for superior flavour — the banana becomes more pronounced and the rum subtler. Decorate with tiny rosettes of cream around the top and bunches of green grapes dusted with icing sugar around the base. Serves 12-14.

Topping
Generously butter base and sides of a 23 cm springform pan. Dust with flour. Sprinkle base with nuts. These will form the topping when the cake is inverted.

Cake
Beat butter, eggs and sugar with electric mixer for 5 minutes until creamy. Beat in alternately the bananas, and the flour mixed with the baking powder. Pour into the pan. Bake 170°C for 55-60 minutes until the centre tests done. Cool; invert onto platter. Prick generously with a fork. Drizzle glaze over top and down sides. Repeat until the glaze is absorbed.

Glaze
Boil for 5 minutes the water, sugar and butter. Remove from heat and add rum.

Topping
1 cup coarsely chopped toasted nuts

Cake
170 g softened butter
3 eggs
1 cup sugar
1½ cups mashed ripe banana
3 cups flour
3 tsp baking powder
1½ tsp vanilla

Glaze
¼ cup water
1 cup sugar
125 g butter
¼ cup rum

Zabaglione Sponge Cake

43

Italy and Austria were once part of the vast Austro-Hungarian Empire. Here again they merge successfully as the ubiquitous Viennese Sponge Cake melds with an Italian filling. 'Zah-bah-glee-oh-nee' is an Italian custard flavoured with Marsala, a fortified wine like sherry. Here it provides a rich golden filling — along with a sprinkle of glacé fruit — between layers of a lemon sponge. The cake is covered with a smooth coating of whipped cream, the top partly covered with more glacé fruit, with a border of piped whipped cream around this centrepiece. A light, most suitable finale to an Italian dinner. The dessert needs at least two hours chilling time, or may be left overnight, but is quick to make and can be simplified further if you use a purchased sponge. Serves 8-12.

Assembly

Bake and cool cake. Slice into three layers. While cake is cooling prepare Zabaglione Filling; whip cream; chop glacé fruit; combine marsala and cream.

Place one cake layer on a serving platter. Sprinkle with about 4 tablespoons of the marsala and cream mixture. Sprinkle with ¼ cup of glace fruit and cover with ½ of the Zabaglione Filling. Top with the second cake layer and repeat as before. Top with third cake layer and sprinkle with remaining marsala and cream mixture. Cover with a smooth coating of whipped cream, leaving a small amount of whipped cream for piping. Sprinkle reserved ½ cup of glacé fruit over the centre of the cake, making a flat even inner circle of it. Surround this with a piped border of whipped cream. Chill at least two hours or overnight.

Viennese Sponge Cake

A smaller version of this cake is used in the recipes for Viennese Ribbon Cake and Strauss Waltz Cake.

Separate eggs while they're cold (they're easier to separate then), putting the whites into a large bowl and the yolks into a small bowl. Allow them to sit at least 30 minutes until at room temperature (warm eggs beat up fluffier).

Beat the whites until soft peaks form, then gradually beat in half the ¾ cup sugar until a very stiff meringue forms.

Beat the egg yolks with the remaining sugar and vanilla until light, pale and doubled in volume. Fold ¼ of the whites into the yolks to lighten the mixture. Fold in the remaining whites. Fold in flour, salt and peel.

Pour into a buttered and floured 23 cm cake pan. Bake at 180ºC (350ºF) for 25-30 minutes. To test, prod the centre of the cake firmly but gently, as soon as it springs back (however hesitantly) remove it from the oven. Do not overbake.

Lightly dust a warm plate with flour. Immediately overturn the cake onto this plate. Let it set there until completely cool. Once cool, remove the pan.

Zabaglione Filling

In the top of a double boiler over simmering water, beat the egg yolks and sugar until well combined. Gradually beat in the ½ cup marsala and lemon juice. Once the mixture is hot sprinkle on gelatine and beat in. Cook for about 5 minutes till thick and creamy. Use immediately or keep warm over hot water.

Combine the ⅓ cup of marsala and the 4 tablespoons of cream. Beat the 1 cup of cream until fluffy. Coarsely chop the glacé fruit, reserving half of it as a garnish.

Viennese Sponge Cake
4 large eggs
½ cup sugar
1 tsp vanilla
¾ cup flour
grated peel of 1 large lemon
dash salt

Zabaglione Filling
6 large egg yolks
¼ cup sugar
½ cup marsala
4 tbs lemon juice
2 tsp gelatine
1 cup glacé fruit or fruit cake mix
1 cup cream
⅓ cup marsala
4 tbs cream

Polish Mazurka Cake

Another easy one, and certain to please: a glistening orange-topped cake served with a sour cream mixture. Accompany with plum brandy and Chopin. Serves 6-8.

Cake
In large mixing bowl beat egg yolks and orange peel until thickened. Gradually add sugar, beating constantly until very thick and creamy. Beat in sour cream. Finely grind nuts and fold into yolks. Beat egg whites and salt until soft peak stage (tips curl over when beaters are lifted). Gently fold into nut mixture. Pour into greased 20 cm springform tin. Bake at 180°C for 35-40 minutes until top springs back when lightly touched. Cool 10 minutes before removing from tin. Top with Orange Topping and Glaze.

Orange Topping
Pierce oranges in several places with a metal skewer. Place in a saucepan with enough water to barely cover. Heat to boiling then simmer gently until oranges begin to soften — about 5 minutes. Remove oranges, cool, then slice 5 mm thick, removing seeds. Meanwhile add sugar to liquid in saucepan. Heat to boiling then simmer gently until a syrup is formed — about 10 minutes. Return orange slices to the syrup and simmer about 10 minutes until the peel is tender and slices are nicely glazed. Remove from heat, strain and cool, before placing on cake. Use the remaining syrup for other desserts or pancakes.

Glaze
Combine sugar and rum and pour over oranges.

Accompaniment
Combine the creams and serve in a side bowl to accompany the cake.

Cake
4 eggs, separated
grated peel of 1 orange
¾ cup sugar
3 tbs sour cream
225 g toasted hazelnuts or almonds
pinch salt

Orange Topping
4 small to medium oranges
1¾ cups icing sugar

Glaze
2 tbs icing sugar
2 tbs rum

Accompaniment
¾ cup sour cream
¾ whipped cream

Hazelnut Caramel Cream Cakes

45

A light, more-ish afternoon tea offering. A simple Cinnamon Hazelnut cake is filled and topped with an equally easy Caramel Hazelnut Buttercream. The cake, baked in a square pan, is sliced into diamond shapes (diagram follows), each one topped with a hazelnut half-dipped in chocolate.

Cinnamon Hazelnut Cake
Coarsely grind hazelnuts and combine with flour, cinnamon and lemon peel. Beat the egg whites in the large bowl of an electric mixer until soft peaks form. Gradually beat in ¼ cup sugar until stiff and sugar is dissolved.

Beat the egg yolks in the small bowl of electric mixer until thick and creamy; gradually beat in remaining sugar and the vanilla until thick and pale. Fold yolk mixture into whites, then gently fold in flour mixture. Spread into a greased, lined and greased again, 20 cm square pan. Bake at 180°C (350°F) for 30 minutes. Turn onto a wire rack to cool. While cooling prepare Buttercream. When the cake is cold slice it in half horizontally; fill with half the Buttercream, top with remaining half.

On one side of the square cake mark it in 3 equal sections; likewise mark the opposite side. On another side of the cake mark it in 4 equal sections; likewise its opposite side. Slice, according to the diagram below, creating 17 diamonds and 14 triangles. Place the diamonds on a serving plate and top each one with a chocolate dipped hazelnut; serve (the triangles are quite edible too!).

Caramel Hazelnut Buttercream
Combine brown sugar and water over low heat until sugar is dissolved. Bring to a boil; boil for 1 minute. Remove from heat, add the 4 tablespoons cream and cool. Beat the butter, vanilla and 2 tablespoons cream until fluffy. Gradually beat in sugar syrup and cinnamon. Stir in ground hazelnuts.

Melt chocolate over hot water. Half dip each hazelnut in chocolate and allow to harden.

Cinnamon Hazelnut Cake
¾ cup roasted hazelnuts
2 tbs flour
grated peel of 1 lemon
1 tsp cinnamon
4 large eggs, separated
½ cup sugar
1 tsp vanilla

Caramel Hazelnut Buttercream
⅓ cup brown sugar, firmly packed
3 tbs water
4 tbs cream
125 g butter, softened
1 tsp vanilla
½ tsp cinnamon
2 tbs cream
¼ cup roasted hazelnuts
17 or more hazelnuts
20 g cooking chocolate

Butterscotch Nougat Slice

For butterscotch fans (amongst whom I number) a novel butterscotch-cum-nougat filling between layers of a simple two-step Walnut Spice Chiffon Cake. The rectangular cake is sliced in half lengthwise and horizontally to create four long thin layers. These are filled, stacked and the top coated with a Cinnamon Glaze. Place a slice on each dessert plate and drizzling Cinnamon Glaze from the tip of a teaspoon, draw a spiral diagonally from one top corner to one bottom corner. Pipe a small rosette of unsweetened whipped cream at the base of the spiral. The glaze is sweet so drizzle a fine trail. Serves 6-8.

Assembly
Bake and cool cake. While cake is baking prepare and cool Custard. Slice cake in half lengthwise, then slice both sections in half horizontally. Place one layer on a serving plate or tray and cover thickly with Custard. Continue layering and filling, leaving top and short sides unfrosted. Frost the two long sides. Chill while preparing Glaze.

Cover top of cake thinly with Glaze. (Gently reheat Glaze if necessary to return to runny consistency.) Chill cake for four hours or longer. Decorate and serve as outlined above.

Walnut Spice Chiffon Cake
Stir together flour, sugar, nuts, mixed spice, Milo and baking powder. Make a depression in the centre of the mixture and add in order: oil, egg yolks, coffee and vanilla. Beat until smooth.

Beat egg whites and cream of tartar until very stiff. Pour egg yolk mixture over whites and fold carefully until just blended. Pour into a 23 cm square pan which has its base greased and floured but not its sides. Bake at 160°C for 30-40 minutes or until the centre springs back when lightly touched. Immediately invert pan onto a wire rack. Allow to cool completely before loosening the sides and removing the pan.

Butterscotch Nougat Custard
Finely chop the nougat reserving about 75 grams. In a small saucepan bring to a boil over medium heat the larger portion of nougat, milk, sugar, and cornflour. Stir constantly to help break down the nougat. Mixture may be lumpy at first but will emulsify. Remove from heat and stir in butter. Once the butter is melted and the mixture is only lukewarm, stir in the remaining nougat (this will give the custard some interesting chewy bits). Cool.

Cinnamon Glaze
Melt butter over medium heat until a light brown. Remove from heat and stir in Milo, cinnamon and icing sugar. Blend in enough hot strong coffee to make a thick but runny glaze. Use immediately.

Walnut Spice Chiffon Cake
1 cup flour
½ cup packed brown sugar
½ cup ground walnuts
¼ cup Milo
3 tsp mixed spice
1½ tsp baking powder
¼ cup oil
3 large eggs, separated
¼ cup + 2 tbs strong coffee
2 tsp vanilla
¼ tsp cream of tartar

Butterscotch Nougat Custard
1½ cups milk
225 g Nougat or French Nougat
2 tbs cornflour
1 tbs brown sugar
100 g butter

Cinnamon Glaze
30 g butter
1 tsp cinnamon
1½ tbs Milo
½ cup icing sugar
3-4 tsp hot strong coffee

Butter Fingers

47

A light lemony yeast dough (don't turn the page you non-bread-makers this one is super quick and simple!) with a baked-on crunchy almond topping. After a brief cooling the square bread is split, filled with a fluffy custard filling, and sliced into gooey fingers. Yummy! If you want more sleek, tidy fingers (the bread ones, not yours) slice the split bread into fingers first then fill. This is OK served the next day but like most sweet doughs is nicest on the day it is baked. Makes 20.

Assembly
Once the dough is fully risen, gently top it with the cooled nut mixture. The dough will deflate somewhat. Allow to rise 10 minutes or more in a warm place while preheating the oven to 200ºC (400ºF). Bake in the top third of the oven for 15-20 minutes until the bread taps with a springy firmness and the topping is browned. Do not overbake.

Leave the bread in the pan until the topping is set. Remove the bread onto a board letting it cool thoroughly, nut side up. Once cool slice it in half horizontally with a serrated bread knife. (If you're in a hurry this can be sliced successfully while still warm, but cool before filling.) Sandwich with Fluffy Custard Filling. Slice gently with a serrated bread knife into 20 fingers.

Yeast Dough
¼ cup plus 2 tbs sugar
½ cup warm milk
1 scant tbs yeast granules
2¼ cups flour
2 tbs butter
1 small egg
1 tsp grated lemon peel

Crunchy Almond Topping
8 tbs butter
¼ cup honey
3 tbs cream
1 cup flaked almonds
½ tsp cinnamon
grated peel of small orange

Fluffy Custard Filling
2 eggs, separated
generous ½ cup icing sugar
¼ cup cornflour
1 tbs sugar
½ tsp vanilla
1 cup plus 1 tbs milk

Yeast Dough
Stir a pinch of sugar into warm milk and sprinkle with yeast. Let stand in warm place (such as on a briefly turned-on burner) for 5 minutes or until frothy. Stir to moisten any dry particles of yeast.

Combine flour and sugar in medium bowl. Melt 2 tbs butter and cool slightly. Lightly beat the melted butter, egg and lemon peel into the yeast mixture. Pour into the flour mixture combining to make a dough. Knead on a lightly floured surface for 5 minutes. Spread into a greased 20 cm pan. Cover and let rise in a warm place (I turn my oven briefly on low to warm then turn the heat off and place dough inside) for 45 minutes or until doubled.

Crunchy Almond Topping
Melt butter and stir in remaining ingredients. Bring to a boil. Cool to room temperature.

Fluffy Custard Filling
Beat egg whites with icing sugar until stiff and glossy. Blend cornflour, egg yolks, granulated sugar, vanilla and a little of the milk in a bowl. Bring remaining milk to a boil in a small saucepan. Stir hot milk into the cornflour mixture. Return to the saucepan and cook for 2 minutes stirring constantly. Remove from heat and fold in beaten whites. Cool.

Ukrainian Date & Poppyseed Cake
with Lemon Custard Filling

Baked in a square pan, sliced in half to form a slim rectangle and sandwiched with a faintly lemon custard filling, this cake is a handsome, homey, darkly dotted winner. Cut into thick gooey slices.

Date and Poppyseed Cake

Choose a 25 cm square pan or something of similar volume — the idea being that once the cake is sliced down its length and layered it will be a pleasing 2-tiered rectangle, not too high and tottery nor too squat and broad.

In a large saucepan simmer the milk until bubbles form around the edge of the milk. Remove from heat and beat in the oil and honey. Stir in dates, poppyseeds, walnuts, vanilla, nutmeg and cloves. Cool mixture to room temperature. Stir in flour and baking powder.

Beat egg whites until stiff and fluffy. Fold carefully into cake batter. Pour into the prepared pan. Bake at 180°C (350°F) for 50 minutes or until a toothpick inserted in the centre comes out dry. Cool the cake for 10 minutes then turn out onto a wire rack to cool completely. Slice the cake down its length to make two equal sections. Trim the tops as necessary so that the layers will fit together evenly. Trim the short edges (which will be the slicing ends of the cake) before frosting. Place one layer on a serving plate and cover thickly with cooled Lemon Custard Filling. Top with remaining layer and custard, drizzling custard down the sides. Sprinkle the top with poppyseeds to form a criss-cross pattern. Allow to sit for a few hours or even overnight to let flavours blend.

Lemon Custard Filling

In medium saucepan combine milk, butter, honey, egg yolks, arrowroot and agar. Bring to a boil then simmer for one minute. Remove from heat. Stir in lemon juice, vanilla and lemon peel (add more peel if you like a sharper lemon taste). Cool to room temperature.

Date and Poppyseed Cake
2 cups milk
1½ cups chopped dates
½ cup poppyseeds
¼ cup ground walnuts
2 tsp vanilla
1 tsp nutmeg
½ tsp ground cloves
½ cup oil
½ cup honey
1¾ cups flour
1 tsp baking powder
4 large egg whites

Lemon Custard Filling
1¾ cups milk
¼ cup butter
¼ cup honey
4 large egg yolks
5 tbs arrowroot
2 tsp gelatine
¼ cup lemon juice
2 tsp vanilla
1½ tsp grated lemon peel

German Rum & Brazil-Nut Cake

49

This is an extravagant cake of German origin. A light buttery quick to make cake is split, sprinkled with rum and sandwiched with a feather-weight buttercream and toasted brazil nuts. More buttercream and nuts coat the cake, and tiny rosettes of frosting may be piped on as a final touch. Keeps and even freezes well. Serve at a special afternoon tea.

Assembly
Toast nuts in butter on top of the stove until golden brown. By hand or in a blender finely chop half of the nuts and coarsely chop the remainder.

Spread buttercream on the bottom and middle cake layers and lightly sprinkle with toasted nuts. Top with the top cake layer and cover the entire cake with buttercream, reserving a small amount for garnishing. Coat top and sides with remaining nuts. Pipe tiny rosettes of buttercream on inner top edge and around base. Chill 30 minutes or longer before serving.

Butter Cake
Preheat the oven to 160°C. Coat the bottom and sides of a 23 cm tube cake pan with 1 tbs soft butter. Sprinkle with the flour, tipping it from side to side, then shake out excess.

In a large bowl cream the 120 g of butter, sugar, 1 tbs of the flour, lemon peel and almond essence. Then beat in the eggs, one at a time and continue to beat until smooth. Combine the remaining flour, cornflour and baking powder and stir this into the batter a little at a time, beating well after each.

Pour the batter into the cake pan and bake in the middle of the oven for 30-40 minutes or until a cake tester inserted in the middle comes out clean. Let the cake cool in the pan for 10 minutes. Turn onto a rack and cool completely. Slice it crosswise into three layers. (The cake may be baked a day in advance.) Sprinkle each layer with rum to an overall total of ½ cup.

Buttercream
Beat the egg yolks until they are thick and lemon coloured; set aside. Cream the butter until light and fluffy.

Bring the sugar, cream of tartar and water to a boil over high heat, stirring only until the sugar dissolves. Boil until it reaches 115°C (236°F) on a candy thermometer, or until a drop spooned into cold water immediately forms a soft ball.

Pour the syrup in a thin stream into the egg yolks, beating constantly with a whisk or electric beater. Continue beating for 4 or so minutes longer, or until mixture is thick and smooth. Gradually add the rum and continue to beat until thick and cooled to room temperature. Now beat in the reserved butter a tablespoon or so at a time. When this is completely absorbed cover the bowl with plastic wrap and refrigerate at least 30 minutes.

Assembly
1¼ cups brazil nuts, almonds or pecans
1 tbs butter

Butter Cake
1 tbs soft butter
2 tbs flour
120 g butter, softened
¾ cup sugar
¾ cup flour
1 tsp grated lemon peel
½ tsp almond essence
4 eggs, at room temperature
½ cup cornflour
2 tsp baking powder
½ cup rum

Buttercream
5 egg yolks
220 g butter, softened
½ cup + 3 tbs sugar
⅛ tsp cream of tartar
⅓ cup water
¼ cup rum

Strauss Waltz Cake

Classically continental this is light enough to leave you waltzing. A Viennese-style fruited spongecake is filled with a quick made-in-the-blender almond cream cheese mixture and topped with toasted flaked almonds. Serve on a paper doily accompanied by Strauss and strong coffee. Note the novel Top Hats variation which follows.

Assembly
Keeping your almond covered cake layer as the top, spread the filling over the other two cake layers, reserving a small portion for piping. Stack the layers appropriately and place on a doily covered serving plate. Pipe tiny rosettes of reserved almond filling on the top outer edge of the cake. Chill one hour or overnight.

Viennese Fruited Spongecake
Separate eggs while cold (this makes them easier to separate) then allow to sit at least 30 minutes to come to room temperature. Warm eggs give greater volume.

Combine flour and dried fruit; set aside. Grease and flour a 23 cm springform pan.

Beat the egg whites until foamy; gradually beat in sugar 1 tablespoon at a time until very stiff.

Beat the egg yolks until thick and pale. Add vanilla and honey and beat for 3-5 minutes until thick. Fold in ¼ of the egg whites to lighten the mixture. Carefully fold in remaining whites. Gently fold in flour and fruit mixture, then fold in melted butter. Pour into pan and sprinkle top generously with flaked almonds to cover. Bake at 180ºC (350ºF) for 45 minutes until centre springs back when lightly touched. Do not overbake.

Remove from oven. Do not loosen sides but immediately invert onto wire rack. If cake protrudes over the top of the pan suspend the pan over the rack by supporting the sides of the pan on two small upturned bowls so that the cake hangs free until cool. Cool thoroughly; remove and slice into 3 even layers.

Almond Cream Cheese Filling
Whizz almonds in blender until finely ground. Add the remaining ingredients and whizz until smooth, adding almond essence to taste.

Top Hats
This is the Strauss Waltz Cake prepared as individual cupcakes or butterfly cakes. They look charming and inviting on a cake platter to both adult and child alike.

Method
Prepare Strauss Waltz Cake batter as before. Pour into well-greased cupcake or fluted individual brioche moulds. Bake for 12-18 minutes. Turn out onto a wire rack; when cool slice out a tidy V-shaped wedge from the top of each cake to a depth of 3-5 cm, almost to the base of the cake. Fill hole generously with Almond Cream Cheese Filling. Spike wedge back into filling and dust the entire top with sifted icing sugar.

50

Viennese Fruited Spongecake
1 cup flour
½ cup finely chopped currants
¼ cup finely chopped dried apricots
6 large eggs
6 tbs sugar
1 tsp vanilla
½ cup honey
¼ cup melted butter
flaked almonds

Almond Cream Cheese Filling
½ cup almonds
1 cup cream cheese, softened
¼ cup sour cream or yoghurt
3 tbs light salad oil
3 tbs honey
1 large ripe banana
dash almond essence

Lemon Twist Torte

51

Striped and set in a springform pan are layers of an easy to make Walnut Chiffon Cake and an equally simple Lemon Apple Mousse. A delicate and not too calorific combination. Remember the Mousse as a Parfait idea: served on its own or alternated with layers of fresh raspberries or cubes of cake.

Assembly
Into a clean 25 cm springform pan place one of the cake layers. Cover with ⅓ of the Mousse mixture and repeat with the Mousse being the final top layer. Chill 3 hours or overnight. Loosen sides with a knife and remove the sides of the pan. Place on serving platter. Pipe ripples of whipped cream around the bottom edge to obscure the pan base. Pipe more ripples on top edge and stud with twists of lemon peel and currants.

Walnut Chiffon Cake
Make the Chiffon Cake as outlined in the Orange Cream Mosaic recipe, adding ¾ cup finely chopped walnuts to the flour mixture and baking the batter in a 25 cm springform pan. Cool completely and slice into 2 layers. The cake may be made the day before if preferred or even frozen well in advance.

Lemon Apple Mousse
In medium saucepan combine the water, egg yolks, arrowroot and gelatine. Boil for 2 minutes until thick. Remove from heat and stir in the lemon juice, peel, apple sauce and currants. Cool to room temperature.

Fold in the sweetened whipped cream. Stiffly beat the egg whites and fold them into the cream mixture. Keep cool — but do not firmly set — while cake is cooling.

Lemon Apple Mousse
2 cups water
3 large egg yolks
⅓ cup arrowroot
2½ tbs gelatine
½ cup lemon juice
1 tbs grated lemon peel
2 cups thick, lightly sweetened apple sauce
½ cup currants
2 cups whipped cream sweetened with 8 tbs icing sugar
3 large egg whites

The Frozen Few

Chewy Chocolate Ice-Cheese Pie

52

A bellissima Italian ice-cream dessert with a crunchy chocolate crust, a double chocolate filling, and a ricotta, mixed fruit and Amaretto topping. When serving remember to let the Pie rest at room temperature for the stipulated time. This results in a frozen chocolate filling, a creamy topping and chewy crust. Well worth the organisation. Freezes well up to a week. Serves 10-12.

Chewy Chocolate Crust

Butter a 23 cm springform pan. Cut a circle of wax paper and fit into the bottom of the pan. Place pan in freezer.

Combine chocolate chips, butter and cream in top of double boiler. Heat until the chocolate is melted, remove from heat and add cinnamon and almonds. Stir until smooth then place saucepan in the refrigerator and stirring from time to time let the mixture cool to peanut butter consistency.

Rapidly spread the mixture into the cold springform pan, over the bottom and up the sides to a height of 3-4 cm. Place pan back in freezer.

Ricotta Filling

Melt the 150 g chocolate over hot water.

Combine ricotta, cream and sugar. Beat until thick but not totally stiff. Stir in Amaretto and vanilla. Spoon half of mixture into another bowl.

To one ½ of mixture add the melted chocolate, cocoa, chocolate chips and cinnamon. Mix well then spoon into the frozen crust mounding it up in the centre so that the filling tapers down as thin as possible at the inner edge of the crust. Replace in freezer.

To the other half of the mixture add the lemon peel, and ¾ cup of the fruit. Mix well. Spread this mixture evenly over the chocolate filling so that the top is flat (this fiddliness is to produce striking diagonal sections of filling when the dessert is sliced). Scatter the remaining fruit over the surface. Freeze.

If you intend to freeze the dessert up to a week, place the pan in a plastic bag and tie securely.

To unmould, let the cassata sit at room temperature for 15 minutes. Run a knife firmly around the edge and release the sides. Lift the bottom of the mould off the dessert then peel off paper. Place the cassata on a serving plate. Pipe rosettes of cream around the edge of the topping. After the torte has remained at room temperature for a total of 40 minutes the individual textures of crust, filling and topping will be perfect. Serve with pride.

Chewy Chocolate Crust
1½ cups chocolate chips
⅓ cup cream
1½ cups finely chopped almonds
4 tbs butter
¼ tsp cinnamon

Ricotta Filling
500 g ricotta or cottage cheese
½ cup sugar
¼ cup Amaretto
2 cups cream
½ cup finely chopped almonds
2 tsp vanilla

150 g cooking chocolate
½ cup chocolate chips
2 tbs cocoa powder
¼ tsp cinnamon

2 tsp finely grated lemon peel
1 cup mixed fruit

1 cup whipped cream for piping

Apricot Pistachio Ice-Cream
with Chablis Ice

53

Pistachios (or other nuts) and pureed apricots are mixed into a homemade or purchased vanilla ice-cream. This mixture is patted up the sides of a decorative mould and the trough created is then filled with a delicate white wine ice. Allow about a day and a half before serving — the assembly is very quick but there are two lengthy freezing times required. Unmould onto a serving plate and garnish the base lavishly with piped whipped cream. Place a fresh or tinned apricot half (concave side up) at intervals and fill the centres with more piped cream. Top each with chopped pistachio nuts. Serves 10-12.

Apricot Pistachio Ice-Cream with Chablis Ice

Chill an 8-cup bombe mould or bundt pan, something rectangular or round with a hollow centre gives the best effect.

Puree the apricots in a blender or food processor. Stir, with the nuts, into the softened ice-cream. Pour into mould and freeze until of spreading consistency (3-5 hours). With a spatula pat the ice-cream evenly against the sides leaving a hollow centre suitable for about 2 cups of filling — the ice-cream can always be squashed down if the cavity ends up being too big. Freeze to firm while you make the ice.

Combine the water, sugar and lemon peel in a small saucepan. Bring to a boil while stirring to dissolve the sugar. Once it has boiled, simmer for 15 minutes without stirring. Sprinkle the gelatine over ¼ cup of the wine in a small bowl. Let stand to soften, about 5 minutes. Stir into hot sugar syrup until dissolved. Stir in remaining wine and lemon juice. Remove peel. Cool to room temperature and refrigerate until thoroughly chilled. Pour into the hollow centre, if necessary patting down ice-cream to make a flat top. Freeze overnight or several days.

To serve, briefly dip mould in hot water. Unmould onto chilled serving plate. Garnish as above. Serve immediately, slicing with a sharp knife.

Apricot Pistachio Ice-Cream with Chablis Ice
- 2 x 500 g tins apricot halves, chilled & drained
- 1 litre vanilla ice-cream, softened
- ½ cup coarsely chopped pistachio nuts
- 1½ cups water
- ½ cup sugar
- outer peel from 1 large lemon, preferably cut in single strip
- 1½ tsp gelatine
- 1 cup Chablis or other dry white wine
- 2 tbs lemon juice
- whipped cream, apricot halves & pistachio nuts for garnish

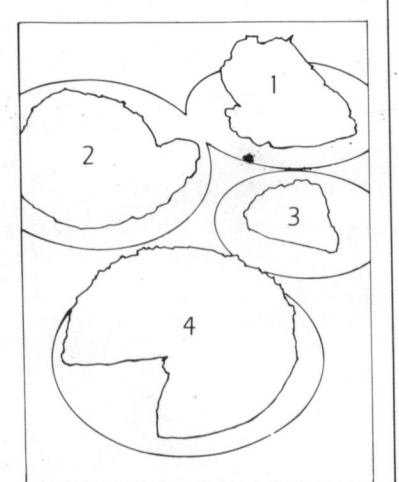

1 French Chocolate Sandwich Loaf (Recipe 58)
2 Orange Cream Mosaic (Recipe 23)
3 Streusel-Topped Poppyseed Cheesecake (Recipe 30)
4 Zabaglione Sponge Cake (Recipe 43)

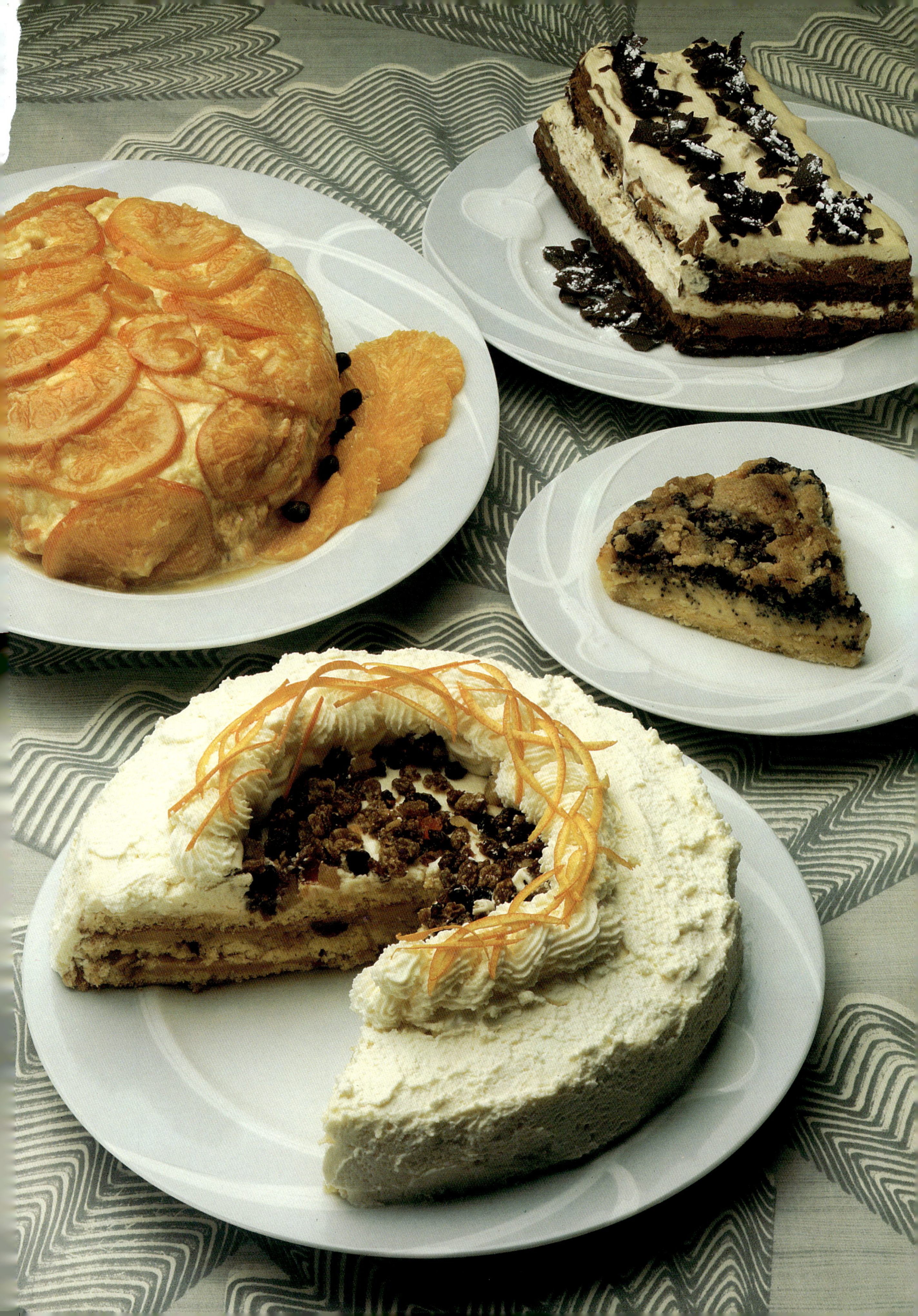

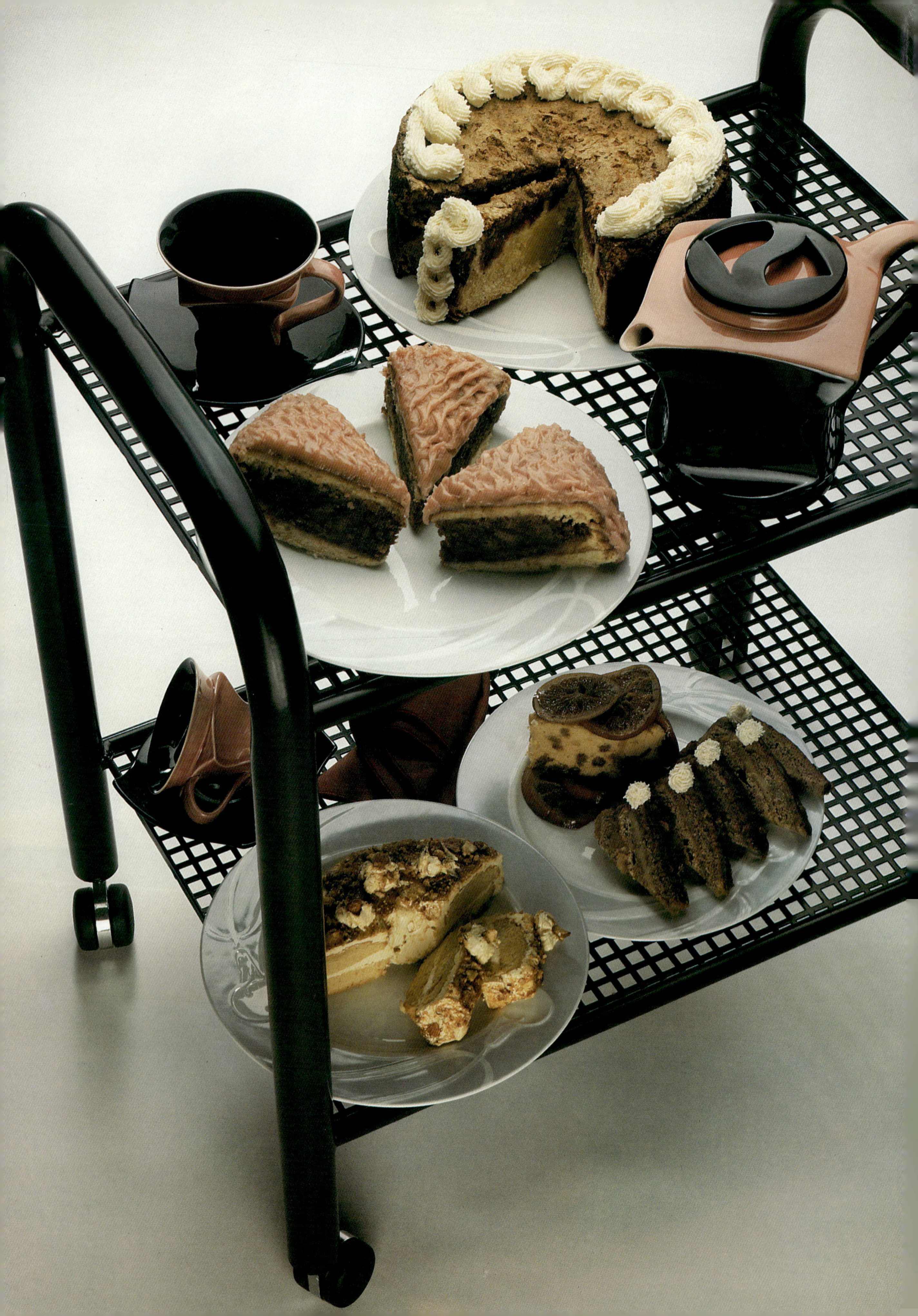

Fig & Almond Ice-Cream

This is so simple to make — no churn or second round of beating required — that you could stop buying ice-cream entirely. The softness of the ice-cream, without the iciness often characteristic of the home freezer product, is due to the high proportion of cream and eggs. Try creating your own flavour variations. This dessert is very attractive set in individual moulds. Turn out onto dessert plates and garnish dramatically. Try topping with fans of black fig and strawberry, say one berry on top and one more plus a fig at the base. Choose large well-shaped fruits with stems intact. Make about four parallel slices from the point to the stem slicing not quite all the way through. Then fan out slices. Serves 8-12.

Fig and Almond Ice-Cream

Soak diced figs overnight in the ¼ cup of liqueur.

Beat 4 egg yolks with ¼ cup sugar adding one tablespoon at a time until thick and creamy. Beat in the 1 tablespoon of Bailey's.

Whisk the 4 egg whites until very stiff then add the remaining sugar and beat for 30 seconds. Whisk the cream until firm but not buttery. Add the yolk mixture, figs, several drops of vanilla, almonds and meringues or macaroons. Carefully fold in egg whites. Pour into one large or small individual moulds and freeze at least six hours.

54

Fig and Almond Ice-Cream
¾ cup diced, dried figs
4 large eggs
600 ml cream
few drops vanilla
¼ cup Baileys Irish Cream
½ cup sugar
1 tbs Baileys Irish Cream
½ cup toasted slivered almonds
3 cups coarsely crumbled meringues (see recipe index) or soft (caky style) almond or coconut macaroons

1 Butter Berry Teacake (Recipe 40)
2 Viennese Ribbon Cake (Recipe 41)
3 Polish Mazurka Cake (Recipe 44)
4 Butterscotch Nougat Slice (Recipe 46)
5 German Rum & Brazil-Nut Cake (Recipe 49)

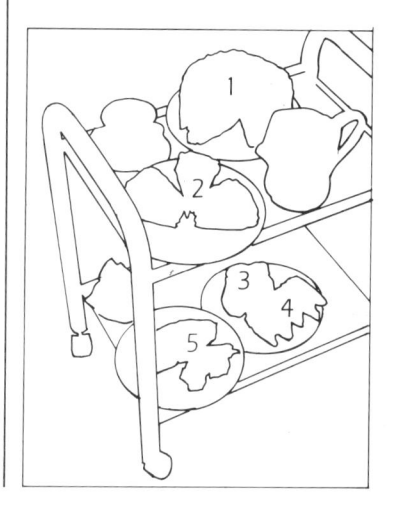

Frozen Chocolate Oranges

55

Intriguing to look at, this is a delicate artistic understatement of a dessert, though super easy to make. Ideal too for preparing ahead of time. Large oranges are hollowed out and half-filled with a quick chocolate mousse, then an orange one. The oranges are frozen then sliced lengthwise into quarters. The quarters can be placed on a serving platter (be sure to turn the odd one on its side to show off the bright orange skin), or three or four segments can be placed on each dessert plate. Pipe a thin rippled line of whipped cream across the demarcation line between the mousses, ending in a rosette of cream at each side.

Frozen Chocolate Oranges

Cut off the tops of the oranges to about a 4 cm diameter. Using a serrated grapefruit knife carefully remove all the flesh and juice from the oranges, leaving the shells intact.

Place the flesh and juice from one orange in a blender or food processor and whizz. Add the icing sugar, honey and liqueur and whizz.

Beat the egg yolks and sugar to a thick 'cream' and divide the mixture into two small bowls. Melt the chocolate and blend into one of the egg mixtures. Fold in half of the whipped cream and pour mixture into the orange shells, half filling them, and freeze.

In a small heatproof cup or bowl heat 1 tablespoon of the orange juice mixture over hot water until very hot. Sprinkle in the gelatine and stir until dissolved. Blend into the remaining egg yolk mixture, then add the remaining orange juice mixture. Chill 40-60 minutes until thick and almost set. Fold in remaining whipped cream and pour into orange shells filling them barely to the top (the filling will expand with freezing). There may be some filling remaining as the quantity necessary is relative to the size of the oranges. Freeze 6 hours or longer. Half an hour before serving remove the oranges to the refrigerator to soften slightly. Slice lengthwise into quarters using a hot knife (dip in hot water then quickly wipe — repeat before each use). Decorate as above. If the dessert is being made well ahead of time: once the filling is firm, wrap the oranges in cling wrap to protect from odours.

Frozen Chocolate Oranges
4 large oranges
¼ cup icing sugar
¼ cup honey
3 tbs orange-flavoured liqueur
2 large egg yolks
2 tbs sugar
60 g cooking chocolate
1 tsp gelatine
1 cup cream, whipped
extra whipped cream for garnishing

Southern Belle Ice-Cream
with Pecan Pastry Fingers

Another easy to make ice-cream, a bit richer and denser than other recipes herein, and lusciously laced with Grand Marnier, honey and dried fruit. The accompaniment is a pastry base topped with a chewy caramel and pecan (or try macadamia) mixture. Serve scoops of ice-cream in small bowls and stud with one or two Pecan Fingers; pass remainder. Easy to make but remember that the ice-cream needs to set overnight. The bars can be made on the day of serving or the day before. Serves 6-8 with extra Pastry Fingers.

Southern Belle Ice-Cream
Combine eggs and half the cream in a saucepan. Stir over low heat without boiling (or it will curdle) until slightly thickened. Remove from heat and stir in honey, cinnamon and orange peel. Cool. Beat remaining cream and Grand Marnier until fluffy. Stir in dried fruit. Fold into custard. Pour into plastic container and freeze for three hours. Lightly whisk with a fork. Return to freezer overnight or longer.

Pecan Pastry Fingers
Pastry:
Place flour in bowl. Cut in or rub in butter until flaky. Blend in egg yolk and lemon juice until mixture will cling together. Form a ball, cover and chill for 30 minutes.

Roll out pastry onto a lightly floured surface into a large enough square to cover the base and fractionally up the sides, of a 20 cm square pan. Cover the pastry with a piece of brown or baking paper and weight with dried beans or rice. Bake at 190ºC (375ºF) for 10 minutes. Remove beans and paper. Bake a further 10-12 minutes until light golden brown and crisp. Cool. When cold, cover with Topping and refrigerate for one hour or longer.

Topping:
Combine sugar, 1½ tbs water, butter and honey in a small saucepan and stir over medium heat until the sugar is dissolved. Bring to a boil, and boil undisturbed for 3-5 minutes until a rich caramel colour. Remove from the heat and blend in the cream. Stir in nuts. Sprinkle gelatine over the 2 tbs hot water and stir to dissolve. Stir into topping.

Southern Belle Ice-Cream
600 ml cream
3 large eggs
½ cup honey
1 tsp cinnamon
1 tbs grated orange peel
½ cup chopped fruit cake mix
3 tbs Grand Marnier or other orange liqueur

Pecan Pastry Fingers
Pastry:
1 cup flour
90 g butter
1 egg yolk
2 tbs lemon juice

Topping:
1¾ cups pecans or macadamias
⅓ cup brown sugar
1½ tbs water
1 tbs butter
2 tsp honey
¼ cup cream
1 tsp gelatine
2 tbs hot water

Pineapple Ginger Ice-Cream Pie

57

A light, creamy tropical tasting ice-cream pie. Super quick to make and consume. Serves 8-10.

Pineapple Ginger Ice-Cream Pie
4 large eggs, separated
1 cup icing sugar
300 ml cream
1 tsp vanilla
450 g tin crushed pineapple
3 tbs diced preserved ginger
½ cup chocolate covered sultanas
extra cream for garnishing
strawberries or pineapple wedges for garnishing

Pineapple Ginger Ice-Cream Pie
Beat egg whites in large mixing bowl until firm peaks form. Gradually beat in icing sugar. Lightly beat egg yolks in small mixing bowl. Fold yolks into whites, then fold in cream. Fold in pineapple, sultanas and ginger. Pour into a 20 cm springform pan which has had its base lined with aluminium foil. Freeze 4 hours or longer until firm. Remove from pan, peel off foil, place on serving plate, and garnish the top edge with piped cream and fresh fruit. Serve in pie-shaped wedges.

French Chocolate Sandwich Loaf

Like French silk knickers under prosaic plaid — don't let the humble name deceive you into underestimating what lies beneath. This easy to prepare frozen loaf is made of layers of chocolate biscuit crust, liqueur cream and chocolate fruit filling. It is an exotic finale to an elegant meal. Serves 8-10, or 6 bent on arterial suicide.

Assembly
Carefully remove chilled crust mixture from pan which has been covered with fruit filling. Cut in half lengthwise. Place one half, crust down, on serving plate and spread with half of the Liqueur Cream. Top with the other crust, crust side down. Spread top only with the remaining Cream and decorate with chocolate shavings (scrape a cold chocolate bar with a vegetable peeler). Freeze the cake. Slice while frozen and let stand at room temperature for 5-10 minutes before serving for creamier, superior taste.

Crust
Combine ingredients into a soft dough. Press into a well-greased slice tray 28 x 18 cm. Bake at 180°C for 15-20 minutes. Cool in tin.

Chocolate Fruit Filling
Melt chocolate and allow to cool slightly. Cream butter and sugar, and add eggs one at a time beating well. Stir in chocolate and dried fruit. Spread over crust and chill at least 1 hour.

Liqueur Cream
Whip cream and liqueur until fluffy.

Crust
1 cup flour
3 tbs cocoa
100 g soft butter
⅓ cup pecans, finely chopped
3 tbs brown sugar

Chocolate Fruit Filling
100 g cooking chocolate
125 g soft butter
¾ cup sugar
2 eggs
½ cup fruit cake mix, finely chopped

Liqueur Cream
300 ml cream
3 tbs Creme de Cacao or other liqueur

Coconut Cloud Ice-Cream
with Raspberry and Port Wine Sauce

59

A light creamy coconut ice with lots of burgundy coloured aromatic fruit sauce to pour over it. Serve in small glass bowls or tall parfait glasses, sprinkle with toasted large coconut flakes, and spike with one or two chocolate finger biscuits or a black liquorice strap cut in two. Serves 6-8 with extra sauce.

Coconut Cloud Ice-Cream

Open the can and pour the coconut cream into a large plastic container. Fill the can with water and pour it into a measuring jug. Make it up to 400 ml with more water. Pour this into a saucepan and add the sugar and salt. Stir over medium heat to dissolve sugar, then boil for 3-5 minutes until syrupy. Cool, then mix the syrup with the coconut cream. Freeze until almost solid, stirring occasionally.

Whip the egg whites until stiff, then gradually beat in the castor sugar. Whip the cream until thick.

Beat the partially frozen mixture thoroughly, then beat in the egg whites. Fold in the whipped cream. Return the mixture to the plastic container and freeze several hours until firm.

Raspberry and Port Wine Sauce

Wash berries and puree in blender or food processor. Combine the puree and sugar in medium saucepan.

Dissolve the cornflour in wine; stir into berry mixture. Cook over medium heat, stirring frequently just until sauce thickens and bubbles. Do not overcook or much flavour will be lost.

Cool to room temperature. Store in a covered container in the refrigerator.

Coconut Cloud Ice-Cream
440 g can coconut cream
400 ml water
½ cup sugar
pinch salt
2 egg whites
¼ cup caster sugar
300 ml cream

Raspberry and Port Wine Sauce
6 cups fresh raspberries or other berries
½ cup sugar
1 tbs cornflour
½ cup port wine

Frozen Coffee & Hazelnut Gâteau

This is fabulous, with layers of nutty meringue, a hint of chocolate and ice-cream. Make two, then one can be kept in the freezer for weeks. It's keeping your family out of the freezer that's difficult. You can take the easy way out and use a purchased ice-cream or make the one-step blender ice-cream (which also has a milk-free version). Serves 8.

Meringue
Reserve 8 whole hazelnuts. Finely grind remainder. Cut two 18 cm circles of greaseproof paper, greased and dusted lightly with cornflour; place on baking trays. Beat egg whites until soft peaks form, gradually add sifted icing sugar and continue to beat until stiff. Fold in half of the ground nuts. Spread meringue evenly over circles. Bake at 160°C for 40 minutes; remove from oven and cool on trays.

Filling
Melt chopped chocolate in top of double boiler. Dip reserved nuts in chocolate to coat evenly and place on sheet of foil to set. Spread remaining chocolate over the flat side of each meringue and allow to set. Place one meringue on serving plate, chocolate side up, spread with slightly softened ice-cream. Place remaining meringue on top with chocolate side down. Return to freezer until ice-cream is solid.

Combine coffee with hot water; cool. Combine cream, coffee and liqueur and beat until soft peaks form. Spread half the whipped cream over the meringue and pipe remaining cream around the top edge. Decorate with the chocolate hazelnuts. Press remaining ground nuts around the sides of the cake and return to the freezer overnight. Remove from freezer 10 minutes before serving.

Banana Chocolate (or Carob) Ice-Cream
Whizz all ingredients except chocolate bars in blender or food processor. Pour into plastic container and stir in chopped chocolate bars. Freeze until firm, several hours or overnight.

*NOTE to freeze bananas place ripe, peeled bananas in a plastic bag and freeze several hours until firm. When blended they go beautifully creamy.

Meringue
- 225 g whole, roasted hazelnuts
- 4 egg whites
- 2 cups icing sugar

Filling
- 170 g dark chocolate
- 300 ml cream
- 1 litre chocolate, nut or hokey-pokey ice-cream or recipe following
- 2 tsp instant coffee
- 1 tsp boiling water
- 3 tbs coffee liqueur

Banana Chocolate (or Carob) Ice-Cream
- 7 large very ripe, frozen* bananas
- 3 tbs maple syrup or honey
- ¼ cup cold coffee
- ⅓ cup oil
- 8 tbs soy or other milk powder
- 3 tbs cocoa or 5 tbs carob
- 1 cup chopped chocolate or carob bars, white or dark chocolate

Lime Cassata Melon Mould

61

Actually this only looks like a melon. A pale green lime ice-cream is semi-frozen in a plastic bowl. Then a rum, dried fruit and nut mixture is pressed on top. After freezing and unmoulding the ice-cream is cut into wedges looking like an inviting darkly stuffed melon slice. Serves 8-10.

Lime Cassata Melon Mould

1½ tsp gelatine
¼ cup lime juice
1 tbs grated lime peel
1 tsp vanilla
375 ml tin evaporated milk, icy cold
pinch salt
dash green food colouring or liquid Chlorophyll
¾ cup icing sugar

1 cup fruit cake mix
¼ cup almonds toasted in 1 tbs butter & coarsely ground
2 tbs rum or Midori melon liqueur
1 tbs cocoa

Lime Cassata Melon Mould

Heat the ¼ cup of lime juice until very hot but do not boil. In it dissolve the gelatine. Stir in the grated peel and vanilla and allow to cool.

Meanwhile beat the icy cold milk until increased in volume and thick like softly whipped cream. Gradually beat in salt, icing sugar, lime juice and food colouring. Pour into a plastic bowl with a narrow base and freeze for 1 hour.

Combine the dried fruit, rum, nuts and cocoa. Press onto the semi-frozen ice-cream, leaving a 3 cm rim free, using more fruit mix at the centre than at the edge. The top of the mixture should now be level, the fruit mix not completely immersed.

Freeze until firm, 6 hours or longer. Unmould and serve immediately cut into wedges.

Strawberry Ice-Cream Brownie Bombe

This super-easy colourfully dramatic dessert combines two of America's (and points southwest) favourite desserts. A bowl is lined with quickly made chocolate brownie cake covered with strawberry jam, filled with strawberry ice-cream, unmoulded onto a base of more chocolate cake and smoothed over with pale pink tinted whipped cream, garnished with fresh strawberries dipped in chocolate. It can keep in the freezer (add the fresh berries later) up to a week. If you ever want to use the brownie recipe on its own, omit the baking powder and you'll have rich fudgy brownies. Serves 12.

Assembly
While cakes are baking, place a 1.5 litre bowl in the refrigerator to chill. When the cakes are cool, line the chilled bowl with aluminium foil. Cut and fit one cake layer to evenly line the inside of the bowl. Spread strawberry jam over the cake. Place in freezer until cold. Wrap second cake layer in plastic wrap; refrigerate. Once the bowl is re-chilled spoon in the ice-cream, packing it down firmly. Smooth top; cover with plastic wrap. Freeze 1 hour or more until firm.

Unwrap the second cake layer; place on serving plate. Remove plastic wrap from ice-cream and unmould onto the cake layer. Remove foil. Return to freezer while preparing the cream: whip cream, sugar and a few drops of red food colouring. Frost bombe with some of the cream to cover smoothly. Pipe remaining cream decoratively up sides and around base. Return to freezer until cream is hard. Garnish top and base with strawberries which have been half-dipped in melted chocolate, and serve.

Chocolate Brownie Cake
In large saucepan heat butter and chocolate just until melted; remove from heat. Stir in sugar, salt and vanilla. Beat in eggs. Stir in flour, baking powder and nuts. Pour into 2 greased and floured 20 cm (8") round cake pans. Bake at 180°C (350°F) for 30 minutes or just until cakes begin to pull away from the sides of the pans. Cool on wire rack in pans until cool. Remove from pans.

Assembly
½ cup strawberry jam
1 litre strawberry ice-cream, softened
2 cups whipping cream
few drops red food colouring — beet juice works remarkably well
¼ cup icing sugar
chocolate-dipped strawberries

Chocolate Brownie Cake
1 cup butter
120 g cooking chocolate
4 beaten eggs
1 cup sugar
2 tsp vanilla
¼ tsp salt
1 cup flour
1 cup chopped walnuts
1 tsp baking powder

Nut & Cherry Tortoni

63

Nut and Cherry Tortoni
3 egg whites
¼ cup water
¾ cup sugar
dash salt
½ cup diced candied or liqueur cherries plus extra for garnishing
¾ cup toasted almonds or other nuts, medium ground
½ tsp almond essence
1 cup cream
1 tsp vanilla

A featherlight, quick to prepare, Italian-style ice-cream flavoured with toasted nuts and candied or liqueur cherries. The mixture is frozen inside pretty paper cupcake liners. Because of their lightness you may wish to accompany them with Coconut Macaroons (see index) or brandy snaps. Serves 6-12 with one or two each.

Nut and Cherry Tortoni
In a small saucepan over medium heat, stir and bring to a boil the sugar and water until the sugar is dissolved. Continue to boil undisturbed, until 110ºC (236ºF) is reached, or a small drop of syrup in cold water forms a 5 cm thread.

Meanwhile beat the egg whites with salt until stiff. Very gradually pour in the hot syrup in a thin stream while continuing beating. Beat until stiff. Cover and refrigerate for 30 minutes.

Beat the cream, almond and vanilla essences, until fluffy. Fold in ½ cup nuts and ½ cup cherries. Fold cream mixture into meringue. Line 12 muffin cups with pretty paper cases. Fill with Tortoni. Sprinkle with chopped nuts and top with a cherry. Freeze several hours or longer.

Simply Superb
quick and easy glamour desserts

Ginger Ripple Log

A beckoningly striated log made with a few basic ingredients. The apples can have a dash of green ginger wine if you wish to be more exotic. Serves 6 or more.

Ginger Ripple Log

On a rectangular serving platter vertically alternate gingernut biscuits with stewed apples and whipped cream which has been flavoured with brown sugar, coffee powder and cinnamon. Spread overall with the whipped cream and sprinkle with more coffee powder, cinnamon and nutmeg. Refrigerate 3-4 hours or longer. Slice diagonally to serve.

Ginger Ripple Log
gingernut biscuits
thick stewed apples with sultanas
whipped cream
instant coffee powder
cinnamon
nutmeg

Cobwebs

65

A delicate cobweb pattern of cream and chocolate is artfully traced on each dessert plate as a background for a simple centrepiece (ideas follow). Serves 4-6.

Cobweb Background

Beat cream and icing sugar until soft peaks form; do not overbeat. Spoon on to individual dessert plates to form a fairly smooth surface. Starting at the centre, drizzle the chocolate in a not too tight spiral over the cream. Then immediately draw a toothpick or fine knife blade from the centre outwards in a spoke-like fashion. This will create the lacy cobweb effect. Top as follows.

Centrepiece
- fresh berries drizzled with liqueur
- scoop of ice-cream coated with chopped roasted nuts
- round piece of cake (use a large glass as a pattern) with fudge sauce or melted chocolate on top

Cobweb Background
1 cup cream
2 tbs icing sugar
30 g melted chocolate

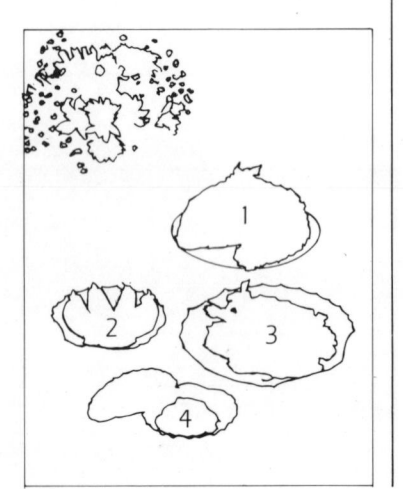

1 Strawberry Ice-Cream Brownie Bombe (Recipe 62)
2 Frozen Chocolate Oranges (Recipe 55)
3 Apricot Pistachio Ice-Cream with Chablis Ice (Recipe 53)
4 Fig & Almond Ice-Cream (Recipe 54)

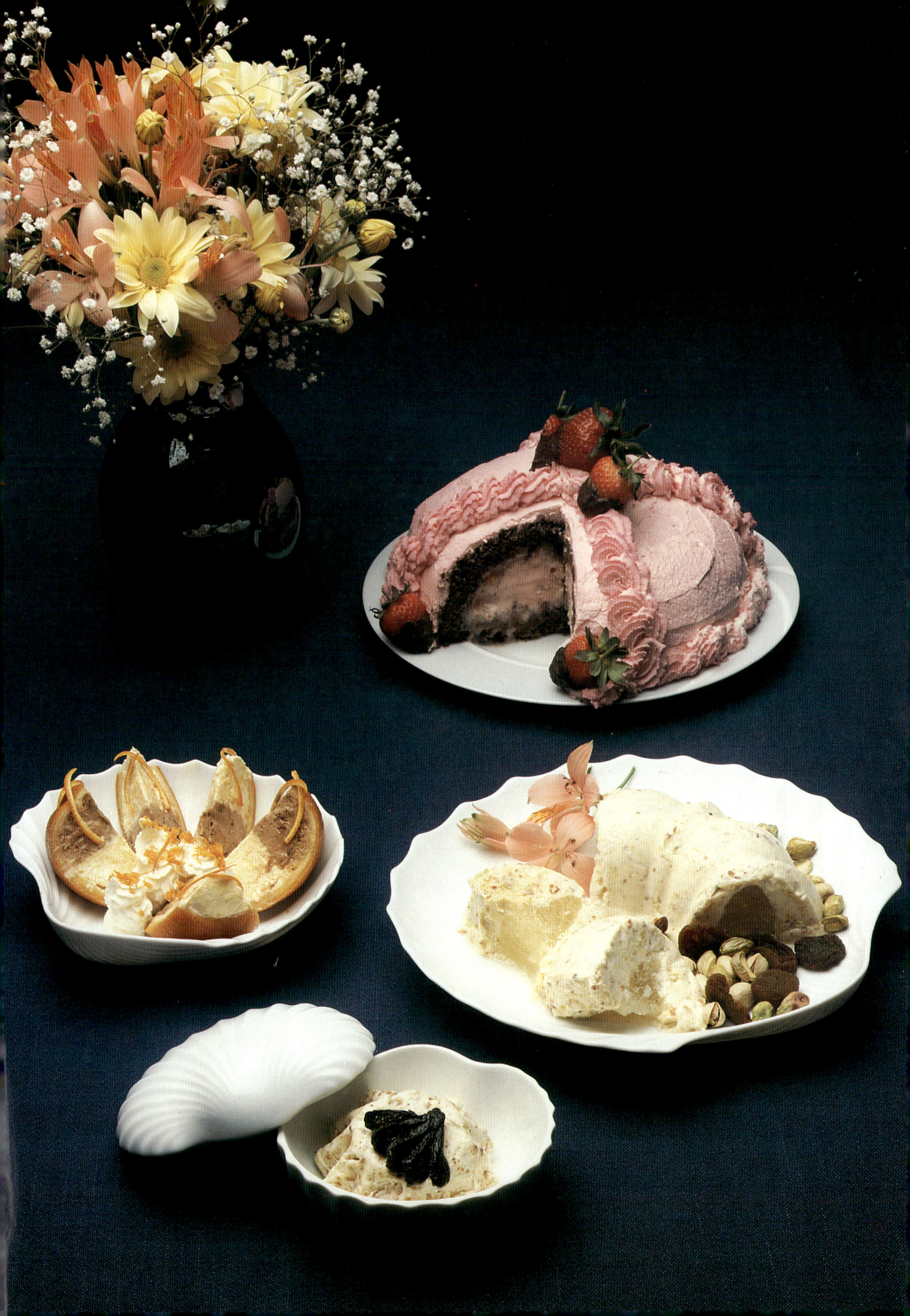

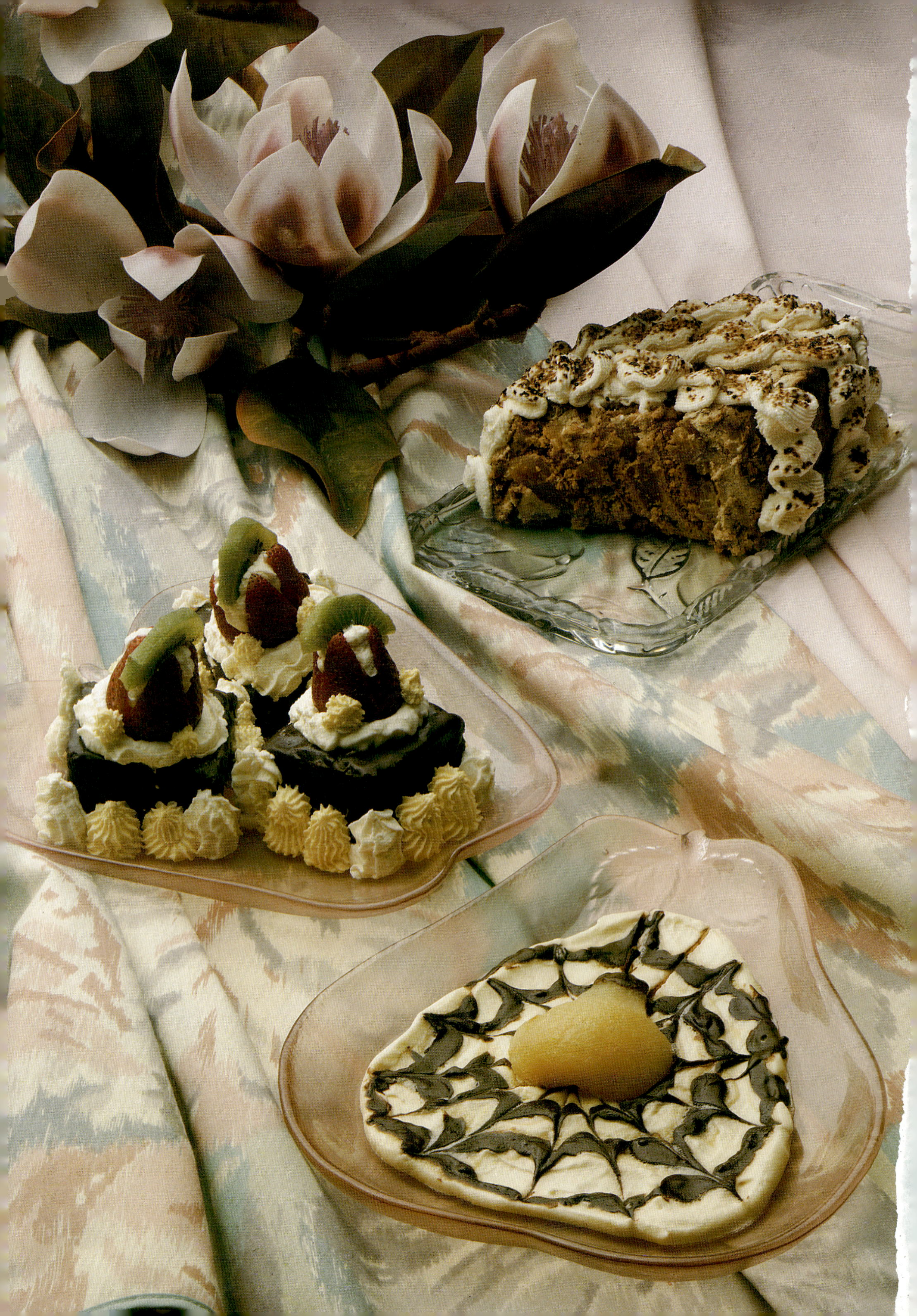

Chocolate Pâté

The name alone induces shudders of delight. A crock of minutes-to-make nutty chocolate spread is accompanied by platters of fresh fruit, mild cheeses, shortbread and semi-sweet wholemeal biscuits. Simple and seductive. Serves 4-6.

Chocolate Pâté
Place the cream in a small saucepan and heat to almost boiling. Remove from heat and stir in chocolate and butter. Allow to cool and thicken. Stir in Amaretto and nuts. Pour into a serving crock and cover. Chill one hour until set or up to several days. Serve with a small butter knife.

66

Chocolate Pâté
180 g cooking chocolate
1 cup cream
3 tbs butter
2 tsp Amaretto or dash almond essence
¾ cup finely chopped toasted almonds or other nuts

1 Ginger Ripple Log (Recipe 64)
2 Strawberry Petit Fours (Recipe 71)
3 Cobwebs (Recipe 65)

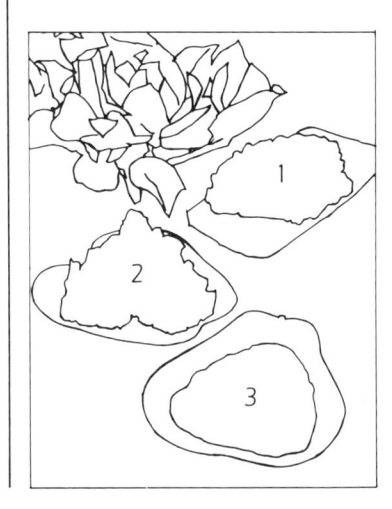

Whole Baked Pineapple

67

Whole Baked Pineapple
1 large ripe pineapple
5 tbs brown sugar
3 tbs rum
3 tbs butter
1 tsp cinnamon
vanilla ice-cream
chopped toasted hazelnuts or
 brandy snaps
hot (not boiled) rum

An exotic 'statement' dessert. A whole pineapple is sliced on one side, its flesh chopped and mixed with a buttery rum and cinnamon mixture and baked in its shell. It's served grandly whole on the table attended by bowls of vanilla ice-cream, topped with chopped toasted hazelnuts or a brandy snap, and a small jug of extra hot rum. Serves 4-6.

Whole Baked Pineapple
Cut a slice from one long side of the pineapple, leaving the green top intact on it. Cut out the flesh inside both pieces of pineapple leaving a strong 10 mm (½") shell. Chop the flesh into bite size pieces and mix with the sugar, rum and cinnamon. Spoon back into the shell and dot with the butter. Set sliced top aside. Wrap filled shell in foil and bake at 180ºC (350ºF) for 20 minutes. Remove foil and replace top on pineapple. Serve immediately on a warm platter. Accompany as above.

Iced Cherry Custard

An appealing summertime refresher. Yoghurt, cream and liqueur cherries are layered in two pink and white stripes and frozen in a fancy mould until firm. Serve with more cherries, the liqueur syrup dripping down the sides, and more whipped cream. Serves 4.

Iced Cherry Custard
Blend the yoghurt with the caster sugar and whipped cream and a dash of almond essence. Combine half the mixture with the chopped cherries and the syrup. Freeze the cherry layer in a lightly oiled decorative 5-cup mould until firm. Cover with remaining mixture and refreeze. Dip the mould almost up to the rim in hot water and invert onto a chilled serving plate. Serve as above.

Iced Cherry Custard
500 g vanilla yoghurt
½ cup caster sugar
300 ml whipped cream
dash almond essence (optional)
½ cup drained, chopped liqueur cherries
2 tbs liqueured cherries syrup
extra whipped cream
extra liqueur cherries for garnish

Banana Orange Sherbets in Shell

69

Banana Orange Sherbets in Shell
3 oranges
1 cup cold custard or sweetened whipped cream
1 cup banana, orange or other complementary fruit yoghurt
2 egg whites
1 ripe banana, mashed
¼ cup sugar
¼ cup + extra banana chips

Oranges are juiced, their half shells frozen and filled with a light banana orange sherbet (if the shells don't stand well on the plate take a tiny slice off the bottom). Cover with toasted banana chips and add a sprig of mint. Serves 6.

Banana Orange Sherbets in Shell
Squeeze the oranges for juice keeping the skins intact. Freeze the half shells. Blend the juice with the custard or cream, yoghurt, mashed banana and ¼ cup banana chips.

Whip the egg whites until soft peaks form then gradually add the sugar to make a firm meringue. Fold into yoghurt mixture. Freeze for several hours, stirring often after ice crystals form, until softly frozen. Serve scooped into shells, garnished as above.

Peanut Butter Ice-Cream Pie

The kids alone will praise you for this one. An unbaked cookie crumb crust is filled with layers of vanilla ice-cream, peanut butter syrup and crunchy toasted nuts. It looks luscious and can be assembled in minutes. Make it in a pie dish or serve rectangular slices out of a square pan.

Cookie Crumb Crust
Combine all ingredients and press firmly onto the bottom and sides of a 23 cm (9") pie dish, making a small rim. Refrigerate until well chilled.

Peanut Butter Ice-Cream Filling
Press half of the softened ice-cream into the pie crust. In a small bowl combine the corn syrup and peanut butter until well blended. Pour half of the mixture over the ice-cream and sprinkle with half the peanuts; top with the remaining ice-cream. Randomly drizzle on remaining syrup mixture; top this with the remaining peanuts. Freeze until firm, about 4 hours.

70

Cookie Crumb Crust
2 cups chocolate peanut cookie crumbs
⅓ cup melted butter
1 tsp cinnamon

Peanut Butter Ice-Cream Filling
1 litre vanilla ice-cream, softened
½ cup light corn syrup or glucose
½ cup creamy peanut butter
¾ cup chopped dry-roasted salt-free peanuts

Strawberry Petit Fours

71

These are elegantly beckoning morsels. Sponge cake is dabbed with Port, filled with strawberry jam, cut into small squares or rounds, and covered with melted chocolate. Large strawberries are sliced into quarters leaving the base intact and filled with piped Port-flavoured cream. Put one or two berries on each cake. Place on a serving platter with any extra berries at random around the plate. There's enough Port Cream to fill 30 large berries.

Port Cream
30 large strawberries
2 egg yolks
2 tbs sugar
3 tbs Port, Marsala or Sherry
1 cup cream
¼ cup icing sugar
2 tbs Port, Marsala or Sherry
extra icing sugar

Cake Base
20-23 cm sponge cake
strawberry jam
¼ cup Port, Marsala or Sherry

Chocolate Topping
200 g cooking chocolate
¼ cup cream

Port Cream
In the top of a double boiler over simmering water, beat the egg yolks, sugar and 3 tablespoons Port until thick and soft peaks form — about 5 minutes. Remove from heat and let stand in cold water, beating until cool. Refrigerate for 30 minutes. Mix together the icing sugar, cream and remaining Port. Blend into egg yolk mixture and beat until stiff. Refrigerate until ready to use.

From their points down, slice each strawberry almost into quarters, leaving the base intact. Chill. Fill with piped Port Cream and dust with icing sugar.

Cake Base
Slice the cake in half horizontally and sprinkle with Port. Spread both sides with jam and sandwich together. Cut into desired shapes and cover with the Chocolate Topping; allow to harden. Place on serving platter and top as above with strawberries.

Chocolate Topping
Melt chocolate in a bowl or double boiler over simmering water. Remove from heat and stir in the cream. Cool slightly before using.

Caramel Peaches

72

A ten-minute caramel sauce turns into a hard nut-brown coating when poured over almond and cream stuffed peaches. Place in a small dessert bowl, pipe lots of whipped cream around the base of the fruit and top with chopped roasted almonds. If you want a more substantial dessert, place a circle of cake in each bowl, soak with liqueur or rum, and top as above with fruit and cream. The coating is very sweet so be sure your other accompaniments are not. Serves 4.

Caramel Peaches
Blanch the peaches by briefly dipping them in boiling water to loosen the skin. Then peel, halve and stone them. Mix the ground almonds with a little of the cream to moisten and fill the peach centres with this mixture; rejoin the halves. Place on serving dishes.

Bring the sugar, milk and butter to a boil, stirring constantly. Simmer for 7 minutes. Pour immediately over the peaches and garnish as above.

Caramel Peaches
- 4 large freestone peaches
- 3 tbs ground almonds
- 1 cup unsweetened cream, whipped
- ¾ cup firmly packed brown sugar
- 5 tbs milk
- 3 tbs butter
- 3 tbs chopped toasted almonds

More Simply Superb Ideas

Recipes which have brief preparation time but require additional baking, chilling or freezing time:
- Marbled Mocha Bombes
- Orange Petal Compote
- Banana Republics (use purchased sponge)
- Fantasy Islands (use purchased meringues)
- Château Royal (use purchased sponge roll and lemon curd)
- Fig and Almond Ice-Cream
- Strawberry Brownie Bomb (use purchased chocolate cake)
- French Chocolate Sandwich Loaf
- Profiteroles
- Zabaglione Sponge (use purchased sponge)
- Chocolate Cookies and Cream Cake
- Lime Cassata Melon Mould
- Pineapple Ginger Ice-Cream Pie
- Frozen Chocolate Oranges

The Finishing Touch

Chocolate Garnishes

Read The First Step chapter for general techniques on working with chocolate.

- Chocolate Leaves —
    - 120 g cooking chocolate
    - 1 tsp oil
    - 5-6 large waxy lemon or orange tree leaves

Carefully melt chocolate and oil. Make sure leaves are dry; using a pastry brush completely coat underside of leaf with a layer of melted chocolate. Hold leaf by the stem and be careful not to brush chocolate onto the top of the leaf which will make the peeling off difficult. Refrigerate briefly until firm, then using stem gently peel off leaf. Use on or around cake, pie, mousse, ice-cream desserts.

- Chocolate Wedges —

Prepare chocolate as for Leaves. On a sheet of wax paper trace a 23 cm circle using the bottom of a cake pan; cut out circle. Place pan bottom side up and moisten with water. Cover with paper circle. With a metal spatula cover paper evenly with chocolate. Refrigerate until firm, about 30 minutes. Heat blade of a long knife in hot water; wipe dry. Quickly but gently cut chocolate into pie-shaped wedges. These are lovely covering a cake. Place a rosette of cream under one long edge (along the outer top edge of the cake) so each wedge is on a slant.

- Chocolate Curls —

Use a square of room temperature cooking chocolate. Draw the blade of a vegetable peeler along the smooth surface of the chocolate. To avoid breaking curls use a toothpick to transfer them.

For an alternative method of making Chocolate Curls, see Amaretto Chocolate Cloud recipe.

- Filigree Chocolate —

Melt 2 squares of cooking chocolate over low heat and drizzle in random spirals over dessert — particularly attractive on ice-cream.

- Cobwebs —

A delicate cobweb pattern of cream and chocolate is artfully traced on each dessert plate as a background for a simple centrepiece of cake or fruit. See Cobweb recipe in Simply Superb chapter.

Fruit Garnishes

- Fondant Dipped Strawberries —
    - 1½ cups icing sugar
    - 1 tbs lemon juice
    - 3 tbs corn syrup or glucose
    - 12 large fresh strawberries

In top of double boiler combine all ingredients. Cook, stirring over hot water until mixture is smooth and thin enough to coat berries. Remove from heat, keeping fondant warm over hot water. Holding berries by hull, dip each into fondant, covering halfway. Place on wire rack to dry.

- Toffee Strawberries —
    - 1 cup sugar
    - ½ cup water
    - 250 g box strawberries

Combine sugar and water in small saucepan, stirring over medium heat to dissolve sugar. Bring heat to high and boil rapidly, uncovered, without stirring, until syrup turns light golden brown; about 5 minutes. Pierce

berries with a skewer, dip into toffee, place on brown paper or foil until set.
- Grape Clusters —
Dip small clusters of grapes or whole berries in beaten egg white, then dip in castor sugar or icing sugar, plain or mixed with coconut, toasted coconut or chopped nuts.
- Fruit Crystals —
Place whole or sliced berries, mint or lemonbalm leaves, orange or lemon segments in ice-cube compartments. Cover with hot water and freeze. Use these clear novelty ice-cubes to garnish frozen desserts (also cocktails, cold soup).
- Fruit Boats —
Serve or set ice-cream or sorbets in halved, hollowed shells of oranges, passionfruit, limes, lemons, avocado.

Other Garnishes

- Gold Threads —
    ¾ cup sugar
    4 tbs water
    pinch cream of tartar

Boil the sugar and water until caramel coloured or 155°C (312°F). Remove from heat immediately; stir in a pinch of cream of tartar. Cool briefly until thick enough to form threads on the prongs of a greased fork. Pull the threads around and over dessert like a magically elevated golden cage. Serve within 30 minutes. Suits simple poached fruit, cream and fruit filled meringue baskets etc.

- Frosted Freesias —
    fresh freesia blossoms
    beaten egg
    castor sugar

Brush freesias with lightly beaten egg, sprinkle with castor sugar and arrange on top of a cake (decoration only). Serve at once.

Component Cooking
How to create your own designer originals.

Component Cooking is an exciting and easy principle to work with: one which helps transform an average cook into an exceptional cook. There are no new physical skills to master, or exotic ingredients to have on hand — the change is made in a moment, in a new expansive way of looking at one's range of possibilities. Where one cook can only see traditional methods and recipes and the prospect of unending repetition thereof, another cook with similar skills and ingredients can create an ever-fresh diversity of simple but stunning meals. How can the switch be made? The answer lies in being aware of the basic formulas and components to cooking, that we all work with, though commonly without recognising them.

One day I was speaking to a friend while she was preparing dinner. I asked her what she was making. She said, 'It's the Potato Corn Croquette recipe from your cookbook (Cooking Naturally). But,' she continued, 'I'm not using potato, I don't have any corn, and they won't be croquettes.'

'Heather,' I congratulated her, 'you are a successful graduate of Component Cooking!'

Heather had learned how to recognise the basic formulas and components which combine to make up any dish, and how to re-structure and re-combine them designing her own original ideas with ease. Thus unnecessary mystique is taken out of cooking and replaced by rewarding, imaginative play in the kitchen. To my mind the so-called average cook is in fact a person of considerable skills. Here is how these existing skills can be vastly enhanced:

Let's look at **sauces and custards** — the basis for many desserts. What are the three absolute requirements to any sauce or custard?

- liquid
- thickener
- flavour

So as long as we have a thickened liquid which tastes good we have a successful sauce (for savoury sauces the principle is the same; for a variety of savoury ideas, see Cooking Naturally.) What are some of the ingredients we can choose from?:

liquids — water, fruit juice, milk (cow, goat, soy), cream, yoghurt and other milk products, coconut milk, liquefied tofu, left-over coffee, white or sweet wines, rum, gin, vodka, liqueurs

thickeners — wheat flour, rice flour, cornflour, arrowroot

flavourings — natural essences, vanilla beans, spices: ginger, cinnamon, mixed spice, nutmeg, anise, cardamom, cloves, allspice, Chinese 5-spice; fresh fruit, dried fruit, coconut and other seeds and nuts, butter and other milk products, grated citrus peel, chocolate and carob, alcohol as above

Using these possibilities (and there are many more) probably hundreds of sauces could be constructed. As an example here is one possible recipe for a Dutch Apple & Date Sauce:

liquid — 2 cups apple/apricot juice
thickener — 4 tbs arrowroot
flavouring — ¼ cup chopped dates
3 tbs brown sugar
1 tsp cinnamon
1 tsp vanilla

Bring all ingredients, except vanilla, to a boil. Simmer 2 minutes, stir in vanilla and serve.

Just as a savoury sauce is in fact the basic component to a soup, stew or casserole, let's look at how a sweet sauce (such as the one above) or custard can be used as a basis for new ideas:

sweet sauce or custard	+ layered with fruit, melted chocolate, nuts, muesli, cake cubes or crumbled cookies	= Striped Parfait
''	+ extra thickener or gelatine* and sliced fruit, poured into pie crust	= Saucy Fruit Pie
''	+ gelatine* and stiffly beaten egg white, folded in	= Mousse or Cold Souffle
''	+ with gelatine* alternated in Springform pan with cake layers	= Gâteau
''	+ whipped cream, frozen	= Ice-Cream

Obviously, in your experimenting, some desserts may not come out exactly as intended! Always have some Emergency Recipe Kit Ideas, such as:

| Trifle or Individual Parfaits | —break up the unsuccessful pie, cake whatever, into attractive individual glasses or a large decorative glass bowl and cover with a quick custard or sauce or ample whipped cream. Decorate with candied cherries or slices of fresh or glacé fruit or melted chocolate or flaked or chopped toasted nuts. If there is time, chill. Serve with pride — don't say a word except to give it an obscure name that no one (hopefully) can challenge you on: Titograd Trifle, or whatever! | |

More ideas with basic recipes:

favourite cake recipe	+ baked in or crumbled into springform pan base. Top with custard (with gelatine*), or mousse or unbaked-style cheesecake mixture. Top with concentric circles of fresh fruit & cover with glaze of 1 cup water brought to boil with 1 tsp gelatine	= Glazed Fruit Torte
favourite cake recipe	+ baked in springform pan and sliced into 2 layers. In clean springform pan alternate layers with mixture of: 4 cups cold custard (with gelatine*), 2 cups diced peaches, ½ cup chopped toasted almonds. Chill until set. Remove sides and decorate top with flaked almonds; around base pipe whipped cream & stud with peach chunks	= Peach & Almond Gâteau

More ideas with basic recipes:

favourite cookie recipe	+ bake mixture as a crust in pie dish or springform pan. Fill with sauce or custard mixed with chopped banana & toasted hazelnuts. Chill until set and cover with 120 g melted chocolate. Pipe rosettes of whipped cream around the edge & top alternately with hazelnuts.	= Banana Hazelnut Cookie Crust Pie or Torte
favourite cookie recipe	+ press into rectangular pan. Top with creamy cheesecake mixture combined with candied cherries & dried pineapple & bake. Serve at room temperature or frozen	= Ice-Cream Bars

These few ideas can help spark your own. One of the most rewarding aspects to my monthly cooking classes is to see people leaving excited, suddenly aware of how inherently capable they are and of how simple creativity is.

Study the recipes in this book and see how a filling from one dessert can be flavoured differently and combined with a crust or cake base from another. Voila, you've just created an original recipe.

*gelatine — 1 tbs gelatine dissolved in a few tbs hot water will firmly set 2 cups of liquid. Custards and sauces are already thickened, so about half that measure of gelatine will softly set a mixture for a mousse, gâteau etc.

Index

All figures refer to recipe numbers

Amaretto Chocolate Cloud 8
Bombes
   Marbled Mocha 2
   Strawberry Ice-Cream
     Brownie 62
Cakes— see also Gâteaux & Tortes
   Almond 39
   Angel Food 26
   Butter 49
   Butter Berry Teacake 40
   Butter Fingers 47
   Butterscotch Nougat Slice 46
   Chocolate 1, 10, 12, 62
   Chocolate Fudge 4, 5
   Chocolate Sponge Roll 13
   Chocolate Stripes 12
   Chocolate Sunset 4
   Cinnamon Hazelnut 45
   Coffee and Hazelnut 60
   Cream, with Chocolate
     Cookies 9
   Date and Poppyseed 48
   Fudge 4, 5
   German Rum and Brazil-Nut 49
   Hazelnut Caramel Cream 45
   Honeyed Hedgehog 39
   Italian Cheesecake 31
   Lord of the Rings 10
   Nut-topped, Rum-drenched,
     Banana Pound 42
   Orange Cream Mosaic 23
   Polish Mazurka 44
   Rum and Brazil-Nut 49
   Sponge 15, 41, 43, 50
   Sponge Roll 13, 37
   Strauss Waltz 50
   Strawberry Petit Fours 72
   Streusel-Topped Poppyseed
     Cheesecake 30
   Turkish Fig and Chocolate 6
   Ukrainian Date and
     Poppyseed 48
   Viennese Ribbon Cake 41
   Viennese Sponge 41, 43, 50
   Walnut Spice Chiffon 46
   Zabaglione Sponge 43
Chilled Desserts
   Amaretto Chocolate Cloud 8
   Candied Peanut and Apricot-
     Filled Meringue Roll 27
   Château Royal 37
   Cherry Cream Gâteau 34
   Chocolate Cookies and Cream
     Cake 9
   Chocolate Fudge Cake 5
   Chocolate Pâté 66
   Chocolate Stripes 12
   Chocolate Sunset 4
   Coffee Velvet 29

Cointreau and Chocolate
   Pots de Crème 11
Fantasy Islands 36
Ginger Ripple Log 64
Irish Cream Pie 32
Lemon Cream and Walnut
   Crisp Sandwich 19
Lemon Twist Torte 51
Marbled Mocha Bombes 2
Marzipan Mardi Gras 13
Orange Petal Compote 14
Peaches 'n' Cream Tipsy
   Torte 26
Polka-Dot Pie 25
Raspberry Rainbow Mould 15
Stilton Mousse 38
Turkish Fig and Chocolate
   Cake 6
Chocolate
   Amaretto Chocolate Cloud 8
   Banana Chocolate
     Ice-Cream 60
   Brownie Cake 62
   Chocolate Sunset 4
   Cobwebs 65
   Cookies and Cream Cake 9
   French Sandwich Loaf 58
   Fruit Filling 58
   Ganache 13
   Garnishes 8, 10
   Glaze 39
   Ice-Cheese Pie 52
   Lord of the Rings Cake 10
   Nut Sauce 26
   Orange and Chocolate
     Profiteroles 28
   Oranges 55
   Pâté 66
   Chocolate and Pawpaw
     Sauce 20
   Chocolate and Pecan
     Topping 16
   Pots de Crème with
     Cointreau 11
   Sponge Roll 13
   Chocolate Stripes 12
   Truffle Torte 1
   Turkish Fig and Chocolate
     Cake 6
Coconut
   Cream Garnish 12
   Ice-Cream 59
   Macaroons 7
Coffee
   Coffee and Ginger Custard
     with Meringues 36
   Coffee and Hazelnut
     Gâteau 60
   Coffee Velvet 29

Marbled Mocha Bombes 2
Mocha Cream 2
Cointreau and Chocolate Pots
   de Crème 11
Cookies, Chocolate, with Cream
   Cake 9
Cream
   Cake, with Chocolate Cookies 9
   Milo whipped 3, 5
   Sour Cream Filling 15
Creams
   Apricot 4
   Caramel 35
   Caramel Hazelnut
     Buttercream 45
   Chocolate Amaretto 8
   Chocolate Buttercream 6, 11
   Chocolate Ganache 13
   Coconut Cream Garnish 12
   Coffee Buttercream 3
   Lemon Curd 19
   Mocha 2, 32
   Orange Pastry 28
   Port 72
   Sour Cream Filling 15
   Vanilla 23, 35
Crêpes
   Banana Creole 21
   Hazelnut, with Praline
     Ice-Cream 20
   Noël 22
Crusts
   Almond and Hazelnut 25
   Chocolate 32, 52
   Cookie Crumb 70
Custards
   Butterscotch Nougat 46
   Chocolate Buttercream 6
   Coffee and Ginger 36
   Fantasy Islands 36
   Iced Cherry 68
   Liqueur 25
   Thick Chocolate 7
Frozen desserts 52-63, 68, 69, 70
Fudge Cake 4, 5
Fillings
   Almond Cream Cheese 50
   Apricot and Candied
     Peanut 27
   Banana 21
   Cheesecake 30, 31
   Cherry and Coconut Cream 34
   Chocolate 10
   Fluffy Custard 47
   Fruit and Cream 18
   Irish Cream Cheese 32
   Lemon Curd 19
   Lemon Custard 48
   Lemon Poppyseed 30

Mincemeat 22
Mixed Fruit and Pecan 33
Pawpaw and Prune 17
Peach and Raspberry 24
Peanut Butter Ice-Cream 70
Prune Liqueur 29
Ricotta 52
Sour Cream 15
Truffle 1
White Wine 37
Zabaglione 43

Frostings
　Chocolate 1
　White Chocolate 12

Fruits
　Apricot Cream 4
　Apricot-Filled Meringue
　　Roll 27
　Apricot Pistachio Ice-Cream 53
　Apricot Purée 35
　Banana Crêpes Creole 21
　Banana Orange Sherbet 69
　Banana Republics 16
　Bananas, Chocolate-Covered 16
　Caramel Peaches 72
　Cherry and Nut Tortoni 63
　Cherry Cream Gâteau 34
　Chocolate Oranges 55
　Fig and Almond Ice-Cream 54
　Fig and Chocolate Cake 6
　Fruited Spongecake 50
　Ginger Ripple Log 64
　Iced Cherry Custard 68
　Lemon Cream and Walnut
　　Crisp Sandwich 19
　Lemon Curd 37
　Lemon Twist Torte 51
　Lime Cassata Melon Mould 61
　Mincemeat Filling 22
　Mixed Fruit and Pecan
　　Tarte 33
　Orange and Chocolate
　　Profiteroles 28
　Orange Banana Sherbet 69
　Orange Cream Gâteau 23
　Orange Cream Mosaic 23
　Orange Petal Compote 14
　Orange Sauce 22
　Oranges, glazed 23
　Pastry Gazebo 18
　Pawpaw and Chocolate
　　Sauce 20
　Pawpaw and Prune Caramel
　　Cream Pie 17
　Peach and Raspberry Cheese
　　Tarte 24
　Peaches 'n' Cream Tipsy
　　Torte 26
　Pears and Macaroons 7
　Pineapple, baked 67
　Pineapple Ginger Ice-Cream
　　Pie 57
　Prune and Pawpaw Caramel
　　Cream Pie 17
　Prune Liqueur Filling 29
　Prune Pie 25

Raspberry and Peach Cheese
　Tarte 24
Raspberry and Port Wine
　Sauce 59
Raspberry Fondant 41
Raspberry Jelly 15
Raspberry Rainbow Mould 15
Strawberry Ice-Cream Brownie
　Bombe 62
Strawberry Petit Fours 71

Garnishes
　Chocolate 8, 10
　Coconut Cream 12

Gâteaux
　Cherry Cream 34
　Coffee and Hazelnut 60
　Orange Chiffon 23
　Orange Cream Mosaic 23
　Turkish Fig and Chocolate 6

Glazes 18, 42, 44
　Chocolate 39
　Cinnamon 46

Ice-Creams
　Apricot Pistachio 53
　Banana Chocolate 60
　Cassata Lime Melon Mould 61
　Chocolate Ice-Cheese Pie 52
　Coconut Cloud 59
　Fig and Almond 54
　Nut and Cherry Tortoni 63
　Pineapple Ginger Ice-Cream
　　Pie 57
　Praline, with Hazelnut
　　Crêpes 20
　Southern Belle 56

Jelly, Raspberry 15
Macaroons and Pears 7

Meringues 8, 16
　Almond 3, 8, 40
　Apricot-Filled Meringue Roll 27
　for Banana Republics 16
　Coconut 27
　Crisp Walnut 19
　Hazelnut 60
　Venus de Milo 3

Mincemeat Filling 22

Moulded Desserts
　Apricot Pistachio Ice-Cream 53
　Château Royal 37
　Fig and Almond Ice-Cream 54
　Iced Cherry Custard 68
　Lime Cassata Melon Mould 61
　Raspberry Rainbow Mould 15
　Strawberry Ice-Cream Brownie
　　Bombe 62
　Three-Coloured Lady 35

Mousses
　Lemon Apple 51
　Stilton 38

Nuts
　Almond and Cherry Tortoni 63
　Almond and Chocolate
　　Sauce 26
　Almond and Fig Ice-Cream 54
　Almond Meringue 3, 8, 40
　Apricot Pistachio Ice-Cream 53

Brazil-Nut and Rum Cake 49
Candied Peanut and Apricot-
　Filled Meringue Roll 27
Hazelnut Caramel Cream
　Cakes 45
Hazelnut Crêpes 20
Hazelnut Meringues 60
Marzipan Mardi Gras 13
Nut and Cherry Tortoni 63
Nut-topped, Rum-drenched,
　Banana Pound Cake 42
Pecan and Chocolate
　Topping 16
Pecan and Mixed Fruit Tarte 33
Pecan Pastry Fingers 56
Walnut Crisp Sandwich 19
Walnut Meringue 40
Walnut Topping 5

Pastry 17, 18, 24, 30, 31, 33, 40
　Choux Buns 28
　Creams — See Creams
　Pastry Gazebo 18
　Profiteroles 28
　Shortcrust 31

Pies
　Chewy Chocolate
　　Ice-Cheese 52
　Irish Cream 32
　Pawpaw and Prune Caramel
　　Cream 17
　Peanut Butter Ice-Cream 70
　Pineapple Ginger Ice-Cream 57
　Polka-Dot 25

Profiteroles, Orange and
　Chocolate 28

Sauces
　Chocolate Grand Marnier 28
　Chocolate Nut 26
　Chocolate Pawpaw 20
　Orange 22
　Raspberry and Port Wine 59

Sherbet, Banana Orange 69
Sponges — See Cakes

Tartes
　Mixed Fruit and Pecan 33
　Peach and Raspberry Cheese 24

Toppings
　Cream Cheese 24
　Chocolate 4, 16, 71
　Coffee Cinnamon 36
　Cream Cheese 24
　Crunchy Almond 47
　Orange 44
　Pecan 16, 56
　Streusel 30
　Walnut 5

Tortes
　Chocolate Truffle 1
　Coffee Velvet 29
　Lemon Twist 51
　Peaches 'n' Cream Tipsy 26

Truffle filling 1